REGIMENTS OF FOOT

Also by H. L. Wickes

REGIMENTS OF HORSE

H. L. WICKES

Regiments of Foot

A historical record
of all the foot regiments
of the British Army

OSPREY

*This book is dedicated to the memory of
my eldest son, the late
Captain Christopher Wickes, R.E.*

Published in 1974 by
Osprey Publishing Ltd., 137 Southampton Street
Reading, Berkshire
© Copyright 1974 H. L. Wickes

Printed in Great Britain by
The Camelot Press Ltd, Southampton

ISBN 0 85045 220 1

PREFACE

In no way does this small book claim to be a history of the British Army: such a subject would necessitate many large volumes. Nor does it comprise a complete record of the memorable battles and campaigns in which the various regiments have been engaged. Rather, it is in the nature of a search for an answer to the question, 'What became of the regiments of foot?'

The last few years have seen the disappearance of many famous regiments, due to amalgamations and the formation of new 'large' regiments. I have endeavoured here to give a brief history of each of the numbered regiments, from its initial establishment to the present-day formation, touching in each case on its origins, traditions, service record and, where appropriate, its most famous engagements. It is said that battles are the punctuation marks of a regiment's history.

Up to about 1750, a regiment when raised was usually named after some royal personage or after the commanding officer. It was in 1743 that the rank or number of regiments was first confirmed by Royal Warrant. The recommendation stated that regiments should take rank from the date of their formation or, if originally raised for service with a foreign power, from the date of their being taken on to the English Establishment.

This numbering of regiments proved reasonably popular, but in 1782 an attempt was made to introduce county titles: this move met with such opposition that it had to be held in abeyance. Regiments preferred to gather their recruits from various large centres of population, rather than limit their recruiting activities to a county area. A second and more successful attempt to introduce county titles was made in the Cardwell Reforms of 1881, and numbers were then officially abolished.

The British Isles were divided into seventy county districts or military areas: each area was allotted an infantry regiment comprising two regular or line battalions and militia battalions – later to be termed 'territorial' battalions. The idea was that one regular battalion remained at home and recruited reinforcements both for itself and the other regular battalion, which would meanwhile be serving overseas. The militia battalions were made up of part-time soldiers, and their purpose was to give support to the regular units in case of war breaking out.

With the Cardwell Reforms of 1881 came the linking of senior and junior regiments as 1st and 2nd battalions – a move which again caused considerable resentment: for example, the 2nd Battalion of the Argyll and Sutherland Highlanders could not tolerate being known as other than the 93rd Highlanders, or by the nickname gained at Balaclava, 'The Thin Red Line'.

Viscount Cardwell, Secretary for War under Gladstone, also introduced many other great reforms for the Army in dress, Colours, short-service and reservist systems, and the abolition of the purchase of commissions.

This book lists 109 regiments of foot. Of these only twenty-eight survive as 'large' or unchanged regiments in the present-day infantry establishment.

Compared with the well-deserved popularity of the Royal Navy and the Royal Air Force, the British Army cannot truly be said to have received its rightful share of public approbation: for centuries it was habitual in times of peace to regard the Army (the licentious soldiery) as the last refuge for misfits and rowdy ruffians not suited to take a responsible place in the established social order. But when it was called upon to fight the nation's battles, the population would pour out its praise for the Army's valour and indomitable fortitude. Kipling sums this up in his poem 'Tommy':

> For it's Tommy this, an' Tommy that, an' 'Chuck
> him out, the brute!'
> But it's 'Saviour of 'is Country' when the
> guns begin to shoot. . . .

Today, the soldier is no longer the pariah of the nation, but a respected fellow-citizen: it certainly does no harm to record a little of the history and tradition of our much-maligned Army. Apart from an exalted record of service and spirit of unity in the ranks, the British Army owes much to the traditions built up over the centuries: each regiment has its own record of past glory which proves valuable in maintaining *esprit de corps* during campaigns.

War is evil and can only be tolerated when the cause is right and just: but no love of peace must be allowed to stifle our admiration of bravery and unflinching heroism. This book touches on some of the most memorable incidents in British military history. We can say with pride that no other army has had such varied campaign experience; no other army can claim such a career of uninterrupted success.

Watton, 1974   H. L. WICKES

CONTENTS

ACKNOWLEDGEMENTS

THE writer is greatly indebted to the curators of the various regimental museums for the generous help so readily given in the checking of facts and details relating to the old regiments of foot. In particular, the writer's thanks are extended to:

Brig.-Gen. B. L. Rigby, C.B.E., The Cheshire Regiment

Col J. M. Clift, The Royal Hampshire Regiment

Col R. D. Maglagan, C.B.E., M.C., The Queen's Own Highlanders

Col N. S. Pope, D.S.O., M.B.E., The King's Own Yorkshire Light Infantry

Col J. M. Forbes, J.P., D.L., The Green Howards

Col B. A. Fagus, O.B.E., The Royal Scots

Lt-Col G. P. Gofton-Salmond, O.B.E., The Sherwood Foresters

Lt-Col A. W. Stansfield, M.B.E., The York and Lancaster Regiment

Lt-Col E. A. T. Boggis, The Duke of Edinburgh's Royal Regiment

Lt-Col R. K. May, The Border Regiment

Lt-Col M. Ryan, O.B.E., The Royal Warwickshire Fusiliers

Lt-Col R. M. Pratt, D.S.O., D.L., The Royal Regiment of Fusiliers

Lt-Col A. C. M. Urwick, D.L., The Somerset Light Infantry

Lt-Col D. V. W. Wakely, M.C., The Dorset Regiment

Lt-Col Brian Clark, Military History Society of Ireland

Lt-Col D. Rogers, J.P., The Queen's Lancashire Regiment

Lt-Col J. D. Ricketts, D.S.O., J.P., The Worcestershire Regiment

Lt-Col J. E. Margesson, M.B.E., The Royal Regiment of Wales

Major D. Baxter, The Northamptonshire Regiment

Major H. A. V. Spencer, The Prince of Wales's Own Regiment of Yorkshire

Major J. F. Ainsworth, The Royal Sussex Regiment

Major J. H. Davis, The Duke of Wellington's Regiment

Major F. J. Reed, The Queen's Regiment

Major E. Jessup, The Royal Anglian Regiment

Major D. T. Tewkesbury, M.B.E., D.L., The Bedfordshire and Hertfordshire Regiment

Major B. W. Baker, M.C., The King's Regiment

Major P. J. Ryan, The Queen's Lancashire Regiment

Major C. R. D'I. Kenworthy, The Gordon Highlanders

Major G. A. N. Boyne, J.P., The Royal Irish Fusiliers

Major J. W. H. Mulligan, The Royal Irish Rangers

Captain A. J. Wilson, The Royal Highland Fusiliers

J. M. Leslie, Esq., The Royal Green Jackets

H. S. R. Case, Esq., The Suffolk Regiment

J. H. Rumsby, Esq., The Durham Light Infantry Museum

J. E. R. Macmillan, Esq., F.S.A. Scot., The Black Watch Museum

W. A. Thorburn, Esq., Scottish United Services Museum

J. A. Daniell, Esq., Leicester City Museum

B. J. Priestly, Esq., Liverpool City Museum

R. Massey, Esq., Dublin City Museum

P. R. Russell-Jones, Esq., Manchester Art Gallery

Without their helpful criticisms and corrections, it would have been virtually impossible to produce this collection of abbreviated histories with any degree of confidence; the disparities encountered in various works of reference only led to confusion.

More detailed historical accounts of the various regiments are available and can be obtained by application to the respective regimental museums. A comprehensive list of the names and addresses of these establishments is contained in *A Guide to Military Museums*, Terence Wise, published by Model and Allied Publications Ltd.

Finally I wish to record my indebtedness to my wife, without whose help and encouragement I could not have undertaken the work this book has entailed.

NUMBERED REGIMENTS OF FOOT

WITH RELATIVE COUNTY TITLES

Designated number	Regiment	Date of raising
1	THE ROYAL SCOTS (THE ROYAL REGIMENT)	1633
2	THE QUEEN'S ROYAL REGIMENT (WEST SURREY)	1661
3	THE BUFFS (ROYAL EAST KENT REGIMENT)	1665
4	THE KING'S OWN ROYAL REGIMENT (LANCASTER)	1680
5	THE ROYAL NORTHUMBERLAND FUSILIERS	1688
6	THE ROYAL WARWICKSHIRE FUSILIERS	1685
7	THE ROYAL FUSILIERS (CITY OF LONDON REGIMENT)	1685
8	THE KING'S REGIMENT (LIVERPOOL)	1685
9	THE ROYAL NORFOLK REGIMENT	1685
10	THE ROYAL LINCOLNSHIRE REGIMENT	1685
11	THE DEVONSHIRE REGIMENT	1685
12	THE SUFFOLK REGIMENT	1685
13	THE SOMERSET LIGHT INFANTRY (PRINCE ALBERT'S)	1685
14	THE WEST YORKSHIRE REGIMENT (THE PRINCE OF WALES'S OWN)	1685
15	THE EAST YORKSHIRE REGIMENT (THE DUKE OF YORK'S OWN)	1685

xxii

THE ROYAL SCOTS
(THE ROYAL REGIMENT)

PRECEDING TITLES

- 1633　Le Régiment d'Hebron or Hepburn's Regiment
- 1637　Le Régiment de Douglas or Douglas's Regiment
- 1666　The Scotch Regiment of Foot
- 1678　Dumbarton's Regiment
- 1684　The Royal Regiment of Foot
- 1751　The 1st, or Royal Regiment of Foot
- 1812　The 1st, or Royal Scots
- 1821　The 1st, or the Royal Regiment
- 1871　The 1st, or The Royal Scots Regiment
- 1881　The Lothian Regiment (Royal Scots)
- 1882　The Royal Scots (Lothian Regiment)
- 1920　The Royal Scots (The Royal Regiment)

TODAY

The Royal Scots is one of the regiments of the Scottish Division.

NICKNAME

Pontius Pilate's Bodyguard

REGIMENTAL MARCHES

'Dumbarton's Drums'
'The Daughter of the Regiment'

By Royal Warrant of 28 March 1633 King Charles I gave authority to Sir John Hepburn to raise a regiment of foot for service with the French. The Scots and the French have been allies on many occasions – some of Joan of Arc's most devoted knights were Scots, and a Scots Guard served the kings of France right up to the eighteenth century.

The 1st Regiment of Foot is the oldest regular regiment of infantry in the British Army, and possibly one of the oldest infantry regiments in the world. Its nickname, 'Pontius Pilate's Bodyguard', is said to have originated in 1643, when the question of precedence was causing considerable rivalry between the French Regiment of Picardy and Douglas's Regiment.

As Lord George Douglas's Regiment, the Royal Scots were lent by King Charles II to Louis XIV of France. From 1675, when the Colonel was created the Earl of Dumbarton, the Regiment played 'Dumbarton's Drums' as its regimental march – and still does so to the present day. Samuel Pepys describes in his *Diary* how much he enjoyed hearing the march played by the Regiment.

The Royal Scots have 137 battle honours, and have served with distinction in all the major engagements of the British Army. At Quatre Bras they earned the praise of the great French Marshal Ney, who referred to them as 'les braves des braves' when in square formation they resisted seven fearsome charges of the French Heavy Cavalry.

The 2nd Regiment of Foot

THE QUEEN'S ROYAL REGIMENT (WEST SURREY)

PRECEDING TITLES

1661   The Tangier Regiment of Foot
1684   The Queen's Regiment
1686   The Queen Dowager's Regiment
1703   The Regiment granted the title 'Royal'
1714   Her Royal Highness, The Princess of Wales's Own Regiment of Foot

1727   The Queen's Own Royal Regiment of Foot
1751   The 2nd or Queen's Royal Regiment of Foot
1881   The Queen's Royal (West Surrey) Regiment
1921   The Queen's Royal Regiment (West Surrey)

TODAY

On 14 October 1959 the Regiment amalgamated with
The East Surrey Regiment (31st and 70th Regiments
of Foot) to form The Queen's Royal Surrey Regiment
which is part of the 'large' Queen's Regiment, of
the Queen's Division.

NICKNAMES

Kirke's Lambs   The Tangerines
The Sleepy Queen's   The Mutton Lancers

REGIMENTAL MARCHES
'Braganza'
'Scipio'
'We'll Gang Nae Mair to yon Toun'

THE 2nd Regiment of Foot was raised in 1661 as The
Tangier Regiment of Foot. The specific objective was to
provide a garrison for that city, and the first Colonel was the
Earl of Peterborough, who had raised the Regiment. (The
Province of Tangier came to Charles II when he was
betrothed to Catherine of Braganza in 1661.)

The Regiment modelled its badge on the Paschal Lamb
taken from the coat of arms of Queen Catherine – it
is also said that the Paschal Lamb signified the Regiment's
sacred mission to battle against the heathen Moors.

Lt-Col Percy Kirke commanded the 2nd Tangier
Regiment (the 4th Foot) in 1680, later becoming Colonel
of the 1st Tangier Regiment (the 2nd Regiment of Foot) in
1682. In 1685 the Regiment had to mete out tough treat-
ment to the Monmouth rebels, which earned it the sardonic

3

nickname 'Kirke's Lambs'. Kirke may have gained an infamous reputation, but he was only carrying out his orders from the Crown and the courts.

During the Marlborough campaign of 1703, the 2nd Foot put up a remarkable resistance lasting some twenty-eight hours against an overwhelming number of French troops at Tongres.

Another nickname was earned in 1811, during the Peninsular War, when the Regiment had the misfortune to allow the French General Brennier and his garrison to escape from investment at Almeida: it acquired thus the name 'The Sleepy Queen's'.

Men of the 2nd Foot were serving as marines in Lord Howe's fleet in 1794 when he won his famous victory over the French off Brest, 'The Glorious First of June'; a naval crown on the Colour commemorates this service.

The 2nd Foot is one of the few regiments to possess a Third Colour: it is now an honorary Colour and is never carried in the ranks on parade.

The 3rd Regiment of Foot

THE BUFFS
(ROYAL EAST KENT REGIMENT)

PRECEDING TITLES
- 1572   The Holland Regiment (service in Holland)
- 1665   The Holland Regiment (service of Charles II)
- 1688   Churchill's Regiment
- 1689   Prince George of Denmark's Regiment
- 1707   Argyle's Regiment
- 1737   Howard's Regiment of Foot
- 1747   (first known as the 'Buffs')

1754   The 3rd Regiment of Foot, The Buffs
1772   The 3rd (Buffs) or East Kent Regiment of Foot
1782   The East Kent Regiment
1881   The Buffs (East Kent Regiment)
1935   The Buffs (Royal East Kent Regiment)

TODAY

On 1 March 1961 the Regiment amalgamated with The Queen's Own Royal West Kent Regiment (50th and 97th Foot) to form The Queen's Own Buffs, Royal Kent Regiment, a component unit of the 'large' Queen's Regiment, which itself is part of the Queen's Division.

NICKNAMES

The Buff Howards	The Admiral's Regiment
The Nut Crackers	The 'Holland' Regiment
The 'Old' Buffs	The Resurrectionists

REGIMENTAL MARCHES
'The Buffs'
'Men of Kent'

THE 3rd Regiment of Foot traces its origin back to a 'Holland' regiment raised in 1572 under the command of Captain Thomas Morgan. It cannot, however, claim seniority to the 1st Foot as it was not taken on to the English Establishment until 1665.

For seventy-five years the Holland regiments – sent to the Netherlands by Queen Elizabeth I – fought and broke the domination of Spain in the Low Countries. It was at the Battle of Zutphen that the great Sir Philip Sydney gave his only bottle of water to the dying English soldier.

From these men came the 3rd Foot; and as the Regiment was originally raised in the City of London, it has the privilege of marching through the City 'with drums beating, Colours flying, bayonets fixed, without let or hindrance and without asking permission'.

The name 'Buffs' appears to have originated from the colour of parts of the uniform or equipment, though which parts of the uniform is in dispute. There were two Colonels called Howard in 1740, and the Regiments of both were named after them. The 3rd Foot took the name 'Buff Howards' to distinguish the Regiment from the 'Green Howards' (19th Foot). The dragon in the badge was probably adopted from a similar figure appearing in Queen Elizabeth's own coat of arms.

The long and distinguished service of the 3rd Foot is part of the history of all the major campaigns of the British Army: their first V.C.s were won in the Crimean War.

In 1906 King Frederick VIII of Denmark was appointed Honorary Colonel of the Buffs, an honour which has been conferred on all Danish monarchs since.

The 4th Regiment of Foot

THE KING'S OWN ROYAL REGIMENT (LANCASTER)

PRECEDING TITLES

 1680 The 2nd Tangier Regiment
 1684 The Duchess of York and Albany's Regiment
 1685 The Queen's Regiment
 1702 The Queen's Marines
 1715 His Majesty's Own Regiment of Foot
 1751 The 4th or The King's Own Royal Regiment
 1867 The 4th (The King's Own Royal) Regiment
 1881 The King's Own (Royal Lancaster Regiment)

TODAY

On 1 October 1959 the Regiment was amalgamated with The Border Regiment (34th and 55th Foot) to form The Kings Own Royal Border Regiment, a regiment of the King's Division.

NICKNAMES
NICKNAMES
Barrell's Blues
The Lions

REGIMENTAL MARCH
'Corn Riggs are Bonny'

THE 4th Regiment of Foot – one of the senior regiments – was raised in 1680 as the 2nd Tangier Regiment, for the express purpose of guarding the dowry of Queen Catherine of Braganza. The first Colonel was Charles Fitz-Charles, Earl of Plymouth, a natural son of Charles II.

In the autumn of 1684 the Regiment received the title 'Duchess of York and Albany's', and when the Duke of York became King James II, the title was accordingly changed to 'The Queen's Regiment'. After the suppression of the Monmouth Rebellion (1685) the Regiment had the unpleasant duty of providing the military attendance on the infamous Lord Chief-Justice Jeffreys during the Bloody Assizes.

It was William III who conferred on the Regiment the 'Lion of England' as its ancient badge, and in 1751 a Royal Warrant authorised the Regiment to bear a 'royal title'. As a result, it wore blue facings and was often referred to as 'Barrell's Blues'. The nickname 'Lions' came, of course, from the badge.

With the accession of George I the Regiment's title had again been altered, this time to 'His Majesty's Own'. This was usually abbreviated to 'The King's Own', which eventually became the title by which we know this Regiment.

The 4th Foot had a long record of outstanding service which included St Lucia (as marines), Gibraltar, the Peninsula, America, Waterloo, the Crimea, the Indian Mutiny, Abyssinia, South Africa and, of course, both World Wars.

7

THE ROYAL NORTHUMBERLAND FUSILIERS

PRECEDING TITLES

- 1674 A Holland Regiment (serving the Prince of Orange)
- 1751 Taken on to the English Establishment as the 5th Regiment of Foot
- 1784 The 5th, or Northumberland Regiment of Foot
- 1836 The 5th, or Northumberland Fusiliers
- 1881 The Northumberland Fusiliers
- 1935 The Royal Northumberland Fusiliers

TODAY

On 23 April 1968 the Regiment was merged into The Royal Regiment of Fusiliers, which is a 'large' regiment of the Queen's Division.

NICKNAMES

The Shiners	The Fighting Fifth
Lord Wellington's Bodyguard	The Old and Bold

REGIMENTAL MARCHES

'The British Grenadiers'
'Rule Britannia'
'Blaydon Races'

1674 saw what was to be the origin of the 5th Regiment of Foot. The new force, to be designated the 5th Regiment in 1751, came from officers and men of a 'Holland' regiment. Soon after this the Colonel was Sir Hugh Percy, later the second Duke of Northumberland, and in 1784 the Regiment was given the second title 'Northumberland Regiment of Foot'.

The long record of service of this famous Regiment includes Gibraltar, the American War, the Peninsula, India, and many other engagements too numerous to enlarge upon here. In 1778 the 5th Foot served as marines in the West Indies (hence the 'Rule Britannia' march); and in the same year at St Lucia they defeated a French force nine times their own strength. To commemorate this victory, a red and white hackle is worn behind the regimental badge.

The 5th Regiment of Foot was one of the few regiments to have a third Colour – a gosling green banner carried by a drummer and paraded on St George's Day to commemorate the battle of Wilhelmstahl in 1762.

The nickname 'The Shiners' stems from the Regiment's high standard of spit and polish in the latter part of the eighteenth century. The 'Bodyguard' nickname was given to it because of its many spells of duty at Wellington's head-quarters. 'The Fighting Fifth' is a justly-deserved tribute to outstanding service in the Peninsular War.

In a Brighton churchyard there is a tombstone which records that one Phoebe Hessel, who died at the age of 101, served as a private with 5th Regiment of Foot in the reign of George IV; however there is some doubt as to whether this is really true.

The 6th Regiment of Foot

THE ROYAL WARWICKSHIRE
FUSILIERS

PRECEDING TITLES

    1675   Vane's Regiment
    1685   Taken on to the English Establishment
    1751   The 6th Regiment of Foot
    1782   The 6th (1st Warwickshire) Regiment

1832   The 6th (Royal 1st Warwickshire) Regiment
1881   The Royal Warwickshire Regiment

In May 1963 the Regiment's title was changed to The
Royal Warwickshire Fusiliers, and in April 1968 the
Regiment merged with other fusilier regiments to form
The Royal Regiment of Fusiliers, which is one of the
'large' regiments of the Queen's Division.

NICKNAMES

The Saucy Sixth   Guise's Geese
The Dutch Guards   The Warwickshire Lads

REGIMENTAL MARCHES
'The Warwickshire Lads'
'McBean's March'

THE 6th Regiment of Foot was raised from a 'Holland'
regiment by Sir Walter Vane in 1674, and though it was
known in 1675 as Vane's Regiment, command was first
given to Colonel Luke Lillingston, the man who later
raised the 38th Foot (The South Staffordshire Regiment)
in 1705.

The long and illustrious service record of the 6th Regiment
of Foot includes such actions as the Battle of the Boyne, the
War of the Spanish Succession, the Peninsular War, South
Africa, the Sudan, and both World Wars.

A Royal Warrant of Queen Anne (1 July 1751) confirmed to the Regiment its ancient badge of the Antelope.
The origin of this badge is very obscure – some say it is taken
from a captured Moorish standard, while others claim it was
brought to the Regiment by Sir Walter Vane, since he was
with the Grenadier Guards, whose 12th Company had an
antelope as a badge. Whatever the truth may be, the
antelope has been retained by the Regiment as a live mascot

– and The Royal Warwickshire Fusiliers is one of only five regiments of the British Army which have an officially authorised live mascot.

King William IV gave the Regiment its Royal title in 1832; and it was in 1852 that a detachment of the 6th Foot stood firm in their ranks, together with other brave troops, when the *Birkenhead* was wrecked off the African coast.

On a lighter note, one Hannah Snell enlisted in the 6th Foot using the name of James Grey; she served with the Regiment (1745), deserted when a flogging punishment was imminent, joined the Marines, and was wounded at Pondicherry (1748). Two years later she revealed her sex and eventually died as a pensioner at Chelsea.

Among the very famous names associated with this regiment are Field-Marshal Viscount Montgomery of Alamein, who joined the Regiment from Sandhurst in 1908, and Field-Marshal Sir William Slim, who joined the Regiment on the outbreak of war in 1914.

The 7th Regiment of Foot

THE ROYAL FUSILIERS
(CITY OF LONDON REGIMENT)

PRECEDING TITLES

 1685 The Royal Regiment of Fuziliers (an Ordnance Regiment)

 1751 The 7th Regiment of Foot (Royal Fusiliers)

 1881 The Royal Fusiliers (City of London Regiment)

TODAY

 In April 1968 the Regiment was linked with: 1. The

Royal Northumberland Fusiliers, 2. The Royal Warwickshire Fusiliers, and 3. The Lancashire Fusiliers (since
disbanded) to form The Royal Regiment of Fusiliers,
which is a 'large' regiment of the Queen's Division.

NICKNAME

The Elegant Extracts

REGIMENTAL MARCHES

'The British Grenadiers'
'Fighting with the 7th Royal Fusiliers'
'De Normandie' (slow)

RAISED by King James II in 1685, the 7th Regiment of
Foot – then the Royal Regiment of Fuziliers – mainly
consisted of 'Tower Guards' of the City of London. As
fusiliers, they were armed with a flint-lock or 'fuzil'; their
first duty was as artillery guards – hence the secondary title
'Ordnance Regiment'.

Lord Dartmouth was their first Colonel; their second, in
1689, the great Duke of Marlborough. Most of the officers
had been specially chosen from other line regiments, so
giving rise to the nickname 'Elegant Extracts'.

In common with other London-raised regiments, the 7th
Foot had the privilege of marching through the City with
'drums beating, Colours flying and bayonets fixed'. Another
privilege granted to the Regiment was that of never
drinking the Loyal Toast in the Officers' Mess; King
William IV (1830–7) had declared that it was totally
unnecessary as the loyalty of the officers of the Royal
Fusiliers was beyond question.

The illustrious service record of this famous regiment
includes the Wars of the Spanish Succession and of American
Independence, the Peninsular War, the Crimea, and a long
list of other engagements too numerous to mention.

On two occasions the Regiment supplied drafts to serve
as marines under both Admiral Byng and Lord Dartmouth;

these past services gave rise to the regimental custom of the band's playing 'Rule Britannia' before the National Anthem.

The 8th Regiment of Foot

THE KING'S REGIMENT (LIVERPOOL)

PRECEDING TITLES
- 1685   Princess Anne of Denmark's Regiment of Foot
- 1702   The Queen's Regiment of Foot
- 1716   The King's Regiment of Foot
- 1751   Eighth, or The King's Regiment
- 1881   The Liverpool Regiment
- 1881   The King's (Liverpool) Regiment
- 1921   The King's Regiment (Liverpool)

TODAY
> On 1 September 1958 the Regiment linked with The Manchester Regiment (63rd Foot) to form The King's Regiment (Manchester and Liverpool). In February 1969 Her Majesty Queen Elizabeth II approved the changing of the title to The King's Regiment, a regiment of the King's Division.

NICKNAMES
> The Leather Hats
> The King's Men

REGIMENTAL MARCHES
> 'The English Rose'   'Zachmi Dil'
> 'Here's to the Maiden   'The Kingsman'
> of Bashful Fifteen'

THE 8th Regiment of Foot was raised in June 1685 by Lord Ferrars and was titled 'Princess Anne of Denmark's

Regiment of Foot'. Consequently, when Princess Anne became Queen of England in 1702, the Regiment was renamed 'The Queen's Regiment'.

In 1714 George I of Hanover became King of England, in 1716 he changed the title of the Regiment to 'The King's Regiment of Foot'. At the same time the Regiment was presented with the badge of the White Horse of Hanover, while the regimental facings were changed from yellow to blue.

It is very difficult to call to mind any of England's major campaigns where the 8th Foot was not represented. Battle honours include Blenheim, Dettingen, Martinique, New Zealand, Alma, Inkerman, and many more. The Regiment's campaigns include the War of American Independence, Egypt under General Abercromby, the Crimea, the Indian Mutiny, and the Burma War.

The 9th Regiment of Foot

THE ROYAL NORFOLK REGIMENT

PRECEDING TITLES

    1685   Cornwall's Regiment
    1751   The 9th Regiment of Foot
    1782   The 9th, or East Norfolk Regiment
    1881   The Norfolk Regiment
    1935   The Royal Norfolk Regiment

TODAY

In 1959 the Regiment linked with The Suffolk Regiment to form The 1st East Anglian Regiment (Royal Norfolk and Suffolk). Later, in 1968, the County affiliations were dropped and the Regiment was totally absorbed in the Royal Anglian Regiment, which is a 'large' regiment of the Queen's Division.

NICKNAMES

| The Fighting Ninth | The Holy Boys |
| The Hungry Ninth | The Norfolk Howards |

REGIMENTAL MARCH
'Rule Britannia'

WHEN James II found himself faced with the rebellion of the Duke of Monmouth in 1685, he raised eight new infantry regiments, one of which (later the 9th Regiment of Foot) was named Colonel Henry Cornwall's Regiment of Foot.

The Regiment first saw service at the Battle of the Boyne in Ireland in 1689, and followed this with the campaigns of the War of the Spanish Succession, the War of American Independence, Corunna, the Peninsula, India, the Crimea – in fact, all the major campaigns over a period of 200 years or more.

At Corunna in 1809, it was a party of officers and men of the 9th Foot which had the melancholy duty of burying Sir John Moore after his death in action.

In June 1935, the Silver Jubilee of King George V, the Regiment was honoured with the distinction of being designated a 'Royal' regiment. By a happy coincidence, this year was the 250th anniversary of its raising.

It is not at all clear how Britannia came to be adopted as the regimental badge: tradition has it that the figure is associated with the battle of Almanza in 1707. During the Peninsular War the Spaniards thought the figure of Britannia was that of the Virgin Mary, so giving rise to the nickname 'Holy Boys'. Official confirmation of the honour and privilege of having Britannia as the regimental badge was given by George III on 30 July 1799.

In World War II, The Royal Norfolk Regiment won five V.C.s, more than any other regiment in that conflict.

THE ROYAL LINCOLNSHIRE
REGIMENT

PRECEDING TITLES

- 1685   Grenville's Regiment
- 1751   The 10th Regiment of Foot
- 1782   The 10th, or North Lincolnshire Regiment
- 1881   The Lincolnshire Regiment
- 1946   The Royal Lincolnshire Regiment

TODAY

In June 1960 the Regiment linked with The Northamptonshire Regiment to form The 2nd East Anglian Regiment (Duchess of Gloucester's Own Royal Lincolnshire and Northamptonshire). Later, in 1968, the County affiliations were dropped and the Regiment was totally absorbed in the Royal Anglian Regiment, which is a 'large' regiment of the Queen's Division.

NICKNAMES

The Springers
The Poachers
The Yellow Bellies

REGIMENTAL MARCH

'The Lincolnshire Poacher'

ON 20 June 1685 King James II commissioned John, Earl of Bath, to raise eleven companies of foot. These, united to the then existing 'Plymouth Independent Company', constituted a regiment soon to be known as the 10th Foot. The command of the new Regiment was given to Lt-Col Sir Beville Grenville, nephew of the Earl of Bath.

Steenkirk (1692), Namur (1694), Blenheim (1704),

Ramillies (1706), Oudenarde (1708), and Malplaquet (1709) are just a few of the engagements where the 10th Regiment of Foot earned great commendation for its valour.

During the War of American Independence it earned the nickname 'Springers' for its quickness and mobility. Services in the Egyptian campaign (1793–1802) earned the Sphinx badge and the battle honour 'Egypt'; and the Peninsular War, the Sikh Wars, the Indian Mutiny, and the Nile campaign were among many occasions where the 10th Foot rendered outstanding service.

On 10 December 1946 His Majesty King George VI gave the Regiment the title 'Royal' in recognition of its long record of noble service.

The 10th Foot have always been closely associated with the 29th Foot (The Worcestershire Regiment), having served with them for many years. The officers of the two Regiments were honorary members of each other's messes, and official letters between them always began 'My Dear Cousin'. On ceremonial occasions, the march of the Worcestershire Regiment was always played before that of the Lincolnshire Regiment.

The 11th Regiment of Foot

THE DEVONSHIRE REGIMENT

PRECEDING TITLES

    1685   The Duke of Beaufort's 'Musketeers'
    1751   The 11th Regiment of Foot
    1782   The 11th (North Devonshire) Regiment
    1881   The Devonshire Regiment

TODAY

    On 17 May 1958 the Regiment linked with The Dorset

Regiment to form The Devonshire and Dorset Regiment, which is a 'large' regiment of the Prince of Wales's Division.

NICKNAME
The Bloody Eleventh

REGIMENTAL MARCHES
'Widdecombe Fair'
'We've Lived and Loved Together'

KING JAMES II raised this Regiment as 'The Duke of Beaufort's Musketeers' in 1685.

The Regiment's badge, showing the castle of Exeter, was originally worn by the Devonshire Militia, and tradition has it that this commemorates the defence of the city of Exeter by county trained bands during the Civil Wars.

The battle honours of this Regiment include Dettingen, Salamanca, the Pyrenees, Nivelle, Toulouse, the Peninsula, Afghanistan (1879–80), and very many more gained in engagements. The 11th Foot earned the nickname 'Bloody Eleventh' in 1808 at the Battle of Salamanca in the Peninsular War, when battle casualties reduced the strength of the Regiment to about 70 men.

The regimental march 'We've Lived and Loved Together' has an interesting story. While marching to action at Salamanca, the 11th found they were marching parallel with a French Regiment. There was no time to halt and exchange fire, so instead the officers exchanged salutes, while the men exchanged ribald remarks as they marched away to battle stations. This was the song sung by the 11th Foot.

In 1831, during riots at Bristol, the 11th (stationed at Cardiff) were ordered to go to Bristol to save the city from pillage and destruction. When sailors refused to take the troops across the Bristol Channel, the 11th seized a ship and took themselves across to save the city.

The 12th Regiment of Foot

THE SUFFOLK REGIMENT

TODAY

In 1959 the Regiment linked with The Royal Norfolk Regiment to form The 1st East Anglian Regiment (Royal Norfolk and Suffolk). Later, in 1968, the County affiliations were dropped and the Regiment was totally absorbed in the Royal Anglian Regiment, which is a 'large' regiment of the Queen's Division.

NICKNAMES

The Old Dozen
The Swede Bashers

REGIMENTAL MARCH

'Speed the Plough'

THE 12th Foot, raised by Henry Howard, seventh Duke of Norfolk, was one of the six 'Minden' regiments. It was in 1759 that the French were decisively beaten at Minden by a numerically inferior Anglo-Hanoverian Army. This event is still commemorated by the wearing of 'Minden' roses on 1 August, the anniversary of the battle.

Another fact of interest is that in 1742 when the Regiment paraded before the King on Blackheath, one of the Colours of the 12th Foot was carried by a young Ensign, 15-year-old James Wolfe – later to be the hero of Quebec.

The 12th Foot won great distinction at Dettingen, well known as the last battle at which a British monarch led his troops into battle in person.

At the siege of Gibraltar (1779–83) the Regiment was granted the battle honour 'Gibraltar' for its services. The 12th Foot had with them during this famous siege their Colours bearing the motto *Stabilis* – they were and are the only line regiment to have a motto *not* granted by Royal Warrant. In 1836 the Regiment was awarded its current motto by Royal Warrant: *Montis insignia Calpe* (the wording on the arms of Gibraltar). Translated this means 'The badge of Mount Calpe', Calpe being a very old name for Gibraltar.

One of the most memorable events in the Regiment's history concerns the wreck of the *Birkenhead* in 1852 – the story of this tragic happening is well known. Of the 350 officers and men who stood fast in the ranks while the women and children took to the boats, some fifty-five young soldiers were a replacement draft for the 12th Foot, then serving in South Africa.

The 13th Regiment of Foot

THE SOMERSET LIGHT INFANTRY (PRINCE ALBERT'S)

PRECEDING TITLES

1685	The Earl of Huntingdon's Regiment of Foot
1751	The 13th Regiment of Foot
1782	The 13th (1st Somersetshire) Regiment of Foot
1822	The 13th (1st Somersetshire) Light Infantry
1842	The 13th (1st Somersetshire) Prince Albert's Light Infantry
1881	The Prince Albert's (Somerset) Light Infantry, later re-titled
	The Somerset Light Infantry (Prince Albert's)

On 6 October 1959 the Regiment linked with The Duke of Cornwall's Light Infantry to form The Somerset and Cornwall Light Infantry, which is part of the Light Infantry of the Light Division.

NICKNAMES

Pierce's Dragoons	The Bleeders
The Illustrious Garrison	The Yellow Banded Robbers

REGIMENTAL MARCH

'Prince Albert's March'

THE 13th Regiment of Foot fought at Dettingen in 1743, and after the Battle of Fontenoy returned to England to take a major part in the Battle of Culloden. As a reward for outstanding service at this latter engagement, the Regiment's sergeants were allowed to wear their sashes over the left shoulder – a distinction normally reserved for officers only.

The 13th were converted to Light Infantry in 1822. In 1838 the Regiment achieved lasting fame for its defence of Jellalabad in the 1st Afghan War. For three long months it beat off the besieging Afghans, but was still able to put on a welcome for the relief force – the regimental band played 'Oh! but ye've been lang o' coming'.

The *London Gazette* of 30 August 1842 announced that Her Majesty had been graciously pleased to honour the Regiment in recognition of the distinguished gallantry displayed in the Burma and Afghan campaigns. The Honours took the form of granting a 'Royal' title, 'Prince Albert's Light Infantry'; changing the Regiment's facings from yellow to blue (the latter being the colour normally reserved for royal regiments); and granting a mural crown superimposed 'Jellalabad' as a badge: this was as a memorial to the fortitude, perseverance, and enterprise shown by the Regiment.

THE WEST YORKSHIRE REGIMENT
(THE PRINCE OF WALES'S OWN)

PRECEDING TITLES
- 1685   Hales's Regiment
- 1751   The 14th Regiment of Foot
- 1782   The 14th, or Bedfordshire Regiment
- 1809   The 14th, or Buckinghamshire Regiment
- 1876   The 14th (Buckinghamshire) Prince of Wales's Own Regiment
- 1881   The Prince of Wales's Own (West Yorkshire Regiment)
- 1922   The West Yorkshire Regiment (The Prince of Wales's Own)

TODAY

On 23 April 1958 the Regiment was combined with The East Yorkshire Regiment (The Duke of York's Own) to form The Prince of Wales's Own Regiment of Yorkshire, which is a 'large' regiment of the King's Division.

NICKNAMES

The Old and Bold	The Rugged and Tough
Calvert's Entire	The Powos

REGIMENTAL MARCHES
'Ça Ira'
'God Bless the Prince of Wales'

RAISED in 1685 by Sir Edward Hales, the 14th Foot took part in the Siege of Namur in 1695. They followed this by garrison service in Ireland until 1715, and after action against the Scottish rebels of 1715–16 they played a distinguished part in the defence of Gibraltar, serving on the Rock until 1742.

In 1745 the 14th Foot were engaged in the Battles of Falkirk and Culloden against the rebel Scots, and after service in the West Indies they campaigned in the War of American Independence (1775). They received their county title in 1782, and fought against the French with great distinction at Tourney and Gueldermalsen. Then followed service in the West Indies, India, and the Far East.

The 14th Foot was one of the regiments that endured the appallingly long-drawn-out siege of Sevastopol in the Crimean War (1855).

The regimental march of the 14th Foot originated from an incident during an action against the French at Famars in 1793. The French troops were singing the revolutionary French song 'Ça Ira', and this was evidently well known to the British. The Commanding Officer, Lt-Col Welbore Ellis Doyle, ordered the regimental band to play the air, saying 'Come on, my lads! We'll beat them to their own damned tune.' Later, the Duke of York directed that the Regiment should adopt 'Ça Ira' as its march – the only regimental march in the British Army gained in battle. The 'Royal Tiger' badge, superscribed 'India', was granted to the Regiment in 1838 for its long service in India (1807–31).

The 15th Regiment of Foot

THE EAST YORKSHIRE REGIMENT (THE DUKE OF YORK'S OWN)

PRECEDING TITLES

    1685   Clifton's Regiment
    1751   The 15th Regiment of Foot
    1782   The 15th or York, East Riding Regiment
    1881   The East Yorkshire Regiment

1935   The East Yorkshire Regiment (The Duke of
        York's Own)

In 1958 the Regiment linked with The West Yorkshire
Regiment (The Prince of Wales's Own) to form The
Prince of Wales's Own Regiment of Yorkshire, which is a
'large' regiment of the King's Division.

NICKNAMES

> The Snappers
> The Poona Guards

REGIMENTAL MARCHES

> 'The Yorkshire Lass'
> 'The 15th Von England' (slow)
> 'The Duke of York'

THE 15th Regiment of Foot fought with great distinction
under Marlborough at Blenheim, Ramillies, Oudenarde,
and Malplaquet (1704–9); and again under James Wolfe
at Louisburg in 1758, and in the following year at Quebec.
The officers of this Regiment wear black 'ground' with their
collar badges and a black line in the gold lace of the full-dress
uniform – all as a memorial to the Regiment's association
with General Wolfe. White roses (the white roses of York)
are fastened to the Colour Pikes on Quebec Day.

During the War of American Independence (1777) the
15th ran short of ammunition at Philadelphia; the Commanding Officer ordered the men to 'snap, and be damned'.
The best shots fired ball ammunition and the rest either
fired blank charges or snapped the locks of their empty
muskets so as to confuse the enemy — hence the nickname
'the Snappers'.

The East Yorkshire Regiment was granted a secondary
title, 'The Duke of York's Own', to mark the Silver Jubilee
of King George V. Not only was 1935 the King's Jubilee,
but it marked the 250th anniversary of the raising of this

famous Regiment. H.R.H. The Duke of York (afterwards King George VI) had been Colonel-in-Chief of the Regiment since 10 October 1922.

The 16th Regiment of Foot

THE BEDFORDSHIRE AND HERTFORDSHIRE REGIMENT

PRECEDING TITLES

1688	Douglas's Regiment
1751	The 16th Regiment of Foot
1782	The 16th, Buckinghamshire Regiment
1809	The 16th, Bedfordshire Regiment
1881	The Bedfordshire Regiment
1919	The Bedfordshire and Hertfordshire Regiment

TODAY

On 2 June 1958 the Regiment amalgamated with The Essex Regiment (44th Foot) to form The 3rd East Anglian Regiment; this is part of the Royal Anglian Regiment of the Queen's Division.

NICKNAMES

The Feather-bedders
The Old Bucks
The Peace Makers

REGIMENTAL MARCHES

'Mandolinata'
'Rule Britannia'
'Mountain Rose'

THE Regiment, raised in 1688, became the 16th Foot in 1751, and in 1872 was allotted the County of Buckinghamshire as its recruiting area: this is alleged to be the origin of the nickname 'The Old Bucks'.

Buckinghamshire has had *two* regular regiments, the 14th and the 16th Foot. In 1809 the then Commanding Officer of the 14th Foot, one Sir Harry Calvert, was the owner of large estates in Buckinghamshire: he arranged an exchange of titles with the 16th Foot, the latter then becoming known as the Bedfordshire Regiment.

At the time of Waterloo the 16th Foot were serving in Canada, and only arrived in Europe in time to take part in the peace parades in Paris: hence, it is suggested, the nickname 'Peace Makers'. This is a little unfair, as there were also three cavalry and twenty-one other infantry regiments that arrived in France too late to fight at Waterloo.

It is also suggested that the real origin of this nickname was the fact that in the 1880s the 16th Foot was the only regiment with Colours unadorned by battle honours. It had had a long period of service in the West Indies and Canada during the time when honours were allowed to be inscribed. The claims made by the 16th Foot for earlier battle honours were not allowed until after 1881: the 'Blenheim' honour, 179 years after the battle! The 'Surinam' honour was awarded in 1898, ninety-four years after Surinam's capture, and 'Namur 1695' in 1910, 215 years after the battle.

The Hertfordshire connection appears to originate from previous associations of the Regiment. In 1873 the Hertfordshire Militia and Hertford Rifle Volunteers were attached to the Bedfordshire Regiment and became the 1st (Herts) Volunteer Battalion. This was really a matter of convenience, as the 49th Hertfordshire Regimental Depot was at Reading.

The addition of the title 'Hertfordshire' was to commemorate the many men of that county who served in the Regiment in World War I.

THE ROYAL LEICESTERSHIRE
REGIMENT

PRECEDING TITLES

    1688   Richards's Regiment

    1713   The 17th Regiment of Foot

    1782   The 17th, or Leicestershire Regiment

    1881   The Leicestershire Regiment

    1946   The Royal Leicestershire Regiment

TODAY

In 1964 the Regiment became the 4th Battalion of The
Royal Anglian Regiment; unfortunately, as the 'junior'
battalion, the Regiment was disbanded in 1970.

NICKNAMES

          The Tigers
          The Lily-Whites
          The Green Tigers

REGIMENTAL MARCHES

          'A Hunting Call'
          'General Monckton' (1762)
          'Romaika'

In September 1688 King James II commissioned Col
Solomon Richards to raise a regiment of foot (later the 17th
Foot), and one of its first duties was to mount a guard at
Windsor Castle.

The War of the Spanish Succession (1702–13), the Seven
Years' War (1756–63), the War of American Independence
(1775–85), India, the Afghan Wars, the Crimea – all these
are among the many campaigns where the 17th Regiment
of Foot won lasting fame and many battle honours.

As a testimony to their outstanding and exemplary service

in India (1804–23), King George IV granted the Regiment the Royal Tiger badge surmounted by 'Hindoostan' (*London Gazette*, 25 June 1835); this can be said to be the origin of the nickname 'the Tigers'.

In November 1946 King George VI gave the Regiment the great honour of granting it a 'Royal' title. The former white facings worn by the Regiment were probably the source of their other nickname.

It was customary for the regimental band of the 17th Foot to play 'Wolfe's Lament' just before the playing of the National Anthem; officers of the 17th, like those of the 15th, 31st, and 47th Regiments, wore a black line in the lace of their full-dress uniform, as a sign of permanent mourning for Gen. Wolfe.

It is sad to record the disbanding of this famous Regiment in 1970; the 'Tigers' are one of many illustrious regiments that have disappeared in the upheavals attending the re-organisation of our modern army.

The 18th Regiment of Foot

THE ROYAL IRISH REGIMENT

PRECEDING TITLES

    1684   Granard's Regiment
    1695   The Royal Regiment of Ireland
    1751   The 18th, Royal Irish Regiment
    1881   The Royal Irish Regiment

TODAY

The Regiment was disbanded in 1922, on the foundation of the Irish Free State.

NICKNAMES

        The Namurs
        Paddy's Blackguards

'Garry Owen'
'St Patrick's Day'

THE 18th Regiment of Foot was the only survivor of nineteen regiments raised in Ireland from Cromwell's Independent Garrison. It was placed on the Irish Establishment as Granard's Regiment in 1684 by Charles II, and brought on to the English Establishment in 1689.

The 18th Foot was the first infantry regiment to receive a distinction for service in battle. For valour and courage at Namur (1695) William III not only granted it the honour of being a Royal regiment, but awarded it the badge of the Lion of Nassau, together with the motto *Virtutis Namurcensis Proemium*: it is from this award that the nickname 'Namurs' originates.

The Regiment fought with outstanding courage in all Marlborough's campaigns, and later all through the War of American Independence. It also fought with great distinction in the China campaign of 1842, and again in the Burma War of 1852-3; in this latter campaign many men of the 18th lost their lives in the jungle and swamps, disease alone claiming the lives of 365 officers and men.

The 19th Regiment of Foot

THE GREEN HOWARDS (ALEXANDRA, PRINCESS OF WALES'S OWN YORKSHIRE REGIMENT)

PRECEDING TITLES

    1688   Luttrell's Regiment
    1751   The 19th Regiment of Foot
    1782   The 19th, or 1st York North Riding Regiment
    1875   The 19th (1st York North Riding, Princess of Wales's Own Regiment)

1882   The Princess of Wales's Own (Yorkshire Regiment)

1902   The Yorkshire Regiment (Alexandra, Princess of Wales's Own)

The Green Howards is one of the regiments of the King's Division.

NICKNAMES
The Green Howards
Howard's Greens

REGIMENTAL MARCH
'The Bonnie English Rose'

As mentioned earlier in this book, prior to 1750 regiments usually carried the Colonel's name. About 1740 there were two Colonels called Howard, one commanding the 3rd and the other the 19th Foot. These Regiments were accordingly known as 'Howard's Buffs' and 'Howard's Greens' respectively, from the colour of their regimental facings. In time the Buffs dropped the Colonel's name, but the 19th became the 'Green Howards' – which title was officially authorised in 1920.

It can truthfully be said that the Green Howards have fought in every quarter of the globe: Spain, the West Indies, Flanders, North and South America, Egypt, the Crimea, the Sudan, Afghanistan, China, and all the widespread campaigns of the two World Wars.

In 1885 the Green Howards were at the Battle of Ginnis, where they defeated the Dervishes. This was probably the last battle where British troops fought in red coats.

In 1875 the Regiment was granted the honour title 'Princess of Wales's Own', Princess Alexandra's husband (later King Edward VII) then being the Prince of Wales. Their badge carried the Princess's personal cypher 'A' entwined with the 'Danneborg' or Dane's Cross. Her late Majesty Queen Alexandra was a Danish princess.

The regimental museum at Richmond, Yorkshire, has on exhibition one of the original muskets issued to the Regiment on its formation, and also one of the original bandoliers with its twelve wooden powder flasks known as 'the Twelve Apostles'.

The 20th Regiment of Foot

THE LANCASHIRE FUSILIERS

PRECEDING TITLES

1688   Peyton's Regiment of Foot
1689   Hamilton's Regiment of Foot
1751   The 20th Regiment of Foot
1782   The 20th, East Devon Regiment of Foot
1881   The Lancashire Fusiliers

TODAY

In 1968 the Regiment merged with three other fusilier regiments (5th, 6th, and 7th Foot) to form The Royal Regiment of Fusiliers. The Lancashire Fusiliers was disbanded the same year.

NICKNAMES

The Two Tens   The Young Fuzileers
The Minden Boys   The Double X's
Kingsley's Stand

REGIMENTAL MARCHES

'The British Grenadiers'
'The Minden March'

IT was on 20 November 1688 that William of Orange

issued a commission to Sir Robert Peyton to raise a regiment of foot. Peyton raised six companies (about 360 men) and was himself appointed the first Colonel of the new Regiment. The Regiment's first county title (East Devon) was taken from its place of raising.

Peyton died in 1689, and Hamilton's Regiment (as it was then called) saw service in Ireland, on Gibraltar (1702), and at Dettingen and Fontenoy.

Dettingen was the Regiment's first association with James Wolfe who, at sixteen years of age, was acting Adjutant to Col Scipio Duroure's regiment. Wolfe was a Major with the 20th at Culloden, and remained with them until 1757 – a total of nine years. Two years later the 20th Regiment of Foot fought at Minden with outstanding skill and bravery. On this occasion the Regiment was commanded by Col Kingsley, a brilliant leader who won great renown for the Regiment and for himself at this battle. 'Kingsley's Stand' became one of the Regiment's nicknames.

Many other famous engagements can be recalled where the 20th earned battle honours, including Corunna and Inkerman (where the Regiment once more delivered the famous 'Minden Yell'); and one cannot omit the famous landing of the Lancashire Fusiliers at Gallipoli in 1915. This heroic performance is summed up by the phrase 'Six V.C.s before breakfast'.

The 21st Regiment of Foot

THE ROYAL SCOTS FUSILIERS

PRECEDING TITLES

    1678   The Earl of Mar's Regiment
    1685   The Scots Fusiliers
    1694   The 21st Regiment of Foot
    1707   The North British Fusiliers

1713 The Royal North British Fusiliers
1751 The 21st, Royal North British Fusiliers
1877 The 21st Foot, Royal Scots Fusiliers
1881 The Royal Scots Fusiliers

TODAY

On 20 January 1959 the Regiment amalgamated with the Highland Light Infantry (City of Glasgow Regiment) to form The Royal Highland Fusiliers (Princess Margaret's Own Glasgow and Ayrshire Regiment), part of the Scottish Division.

NICKNAMES

The Earl of Mar's Grey Breeks
Marlborough's Own

REGIMENTAL MARCH

'The British Grenadiers'

ON 23 September 1678 Charles Erskine, fifth Earl of Mar, was commissioned to raise a regiment of foot. The history of this famous fighting unit reads almost like a record of the nation's military engagements.

Originally they were engaged in maintaining peace and order in Scotland (1678–87), and then followed the campaign in the Netherlands, where the 21st Foot fought at Walcourt (1689), Steenkirk (1692), and Landen (1693).

During the War of the Spanish Succession, the Regiment justly earned the nickname 'Marlborough's Own' by their magnificent display of courage and endurance at Blenheim, Ramillies, Oudenarde, Malplaquet, and Bouchain (1704–11).

As the Royal North British Fusiliers the Regiment was at Dettingen (1743) and Fontenoy (1745). It fought at Gibraltar, in the War of American Independence, the Napoleonic Wars – in fact it is difficult to find any major engagement where the Regiment was not represented.

33

In all, the Royal Highland Fusiliers (of which the Royal Scots Fusiliers can be said to be a parent regiment) have more than 200 battle honours, a record not exceeded by any regiment in the British Army.

The 22nd Regiment of Foot

THE CHESHIRE REGIMENT

PRECEDING TITLES

    1689   The Duke of Norfolk's Regiment of Foot

    1751   The 22nd Regiment of Foot

    1782   The 22nd (Cheshire) Regiment

    1881   The Cheshire Regiment

TODAY

    The Regiment is part of the Prince of Wales's Division.

NICKNAMES

        The Old Two Twos
        The Red Knights
        The Lightning Conductors

REGIMENTAL MARCHES

        'The Young May   'Sambre et Meuse'
            Moon'   'Wha Wadna Fecht for
        'Come Lasses and   Charlie?'
            Lads'

In 1689 several new regiments were raised to resist the attempt by the former King James II to regain the English throne. One of these regiments was raised by Henry, Duke of Norfolk, on the Wirral Peninsula, and this was later numbered the 22nd Regiment of Foot.

Its first action was at the Siege of Carrickfergus, followed by the Battle of the Boyne and the capture of Athlone (1691). Next followed campaigns in Jamaica and Minorca (1726), and the Battle of Dettingen (1743).

It was at this latter action that men of the 22nd Regiment saved King George II from capture. Tradition has it that His Majesty plucked a twig from an oak tree and expressed the wish that this might be the Regiment's badge. Hence the acorn design worn by the Regiment, and the tradition of the wearing of an oak-leaf in the head-dress in the presence of royalty.

Many other campaigns can be included in the long service list of the 22nd Regiment of Foot – Canada, America, South Africa, India, Mauritius, Burma, and both World Wars.

The 23rd Regiment of Foot

THE ROYAL WELCH FUSILIERS

PRECEDING TITLES

1689	Lord Herbert's Regiment
1694	Ingoldsby's Regiment
1714	The 23rd, The Prince of Wales's Own Royal Welsh Fusiliers
1727	The 23rd Royal Welsh Fusiliers
1881	The Royal Welsh Fusiliers
1920	The Royal Welch Fusiliers

TODAY

The Regiment is part of the Prince of Wales's Division.

NICKNAMES

The Nanny Goats
The Royal Goats
The Flash

35

'The British Grenadiers'
'Men of Harlech'

THE 23rd Foot was originally raised by Henry, Lord Herbert, in Wales and adjacent counties in March 1689; headquarters were at Ludlow in Shropshire, and the first Colonel was Charles Herbert, a relative of Lord Herbert.

The Regiment took part in the Battle of the Boyne in Ireland (1690), and fought at Namur in 1695, and under Marlborough at Blenheim, Ramillies, Oudenarde, and Malplaquet.

The 23rd were at Minden in 1759, and at Bunker's Hill and Brandywine in America (1775-7). They were the first troops to land in Egypt in 1801, and the last to embark at Corunna in 1809.

In the Peninsula the 23rd won many battle honours, and later fought at Wellington's last great victory, Waterloo. In the Crimean War Sgt Luke O'Connor won one of the earliest V.C.s. He was commissioned and later became a General.

On 1 March, St David's Day, all ranks of the 23rd wear leeks in their headgear, and the custom of 'eating the leek' is observed in the Officers' Mess by those officers who have not previously done so.

The 'flash', a bunch of black ribbon which is a relic of the pigtail, used to be worn as a dress distinction by officers of the 23rd. Permission to wear the 'flash' was extended to all ranks of the Regiment in 1900.

'Her Majesty's Goat', under the supervision of a 'Goat Major', takes his place in regimental parades. The horns of the goat are encased in polished brass and a silver plate on his forehead is inscribed with the sovereign's name.

The present spelling 'Welch' was adopted in 1920 (Army Order 56 of 1920).

The 24th Regiment of Foot

THE SOUTH WALES BORDERERS

TODAY

In June 1969 the Regiment linked with The Welch Regiment to form The Royal Regiment of Wales, which is a 'large' regiment of the Prince of Wales's Division.

NICKNAMES

Howard's Greens
The Bengal Tigers

REGIMENTAL MARCHES

'Men of Harlech'
'The Warwickshire Lads'

SIR EDWARD DERING, of Surrenden in Kent, raised this Regiment in 1689 at the request of King William III, and it has a very long and distinguished record of service in many campaigns, among which can be named Blenheim (1704), the Seven Years' War, the War of American Independence (1775), Egypt, the Peninsular War, and many others.

Its long service in India earned the Regiment the nickname 'Bengal Tigers'; the name 'Howard's Greens' (1717–37) arose when Col Howard was the Commanding Officer and the Regiment wore green facings. A considerable number of Warwickshire men were recruited into the 24th Foot in the latter part of the eighteenth century – hence 'Warwickshire Lads' as one of the regimental marches.

37

The regimental Colours bear a wreath of immortelles granted by Queen Victoria in 1880 in recognition of heroic actions at Isandhlwana and Rorke's Drift, in the Zulu War (1878–9). The Regiment lost twenty-one officers and 590 men at the first of these actions, but more than a thousand Zulus died. Lt Smith-Dorrien (afterwards Gen. Sir Horace Smith-Dorrien of Le Cateau) was one of the survivors of the battle, but Lts Melville and Coghill died in a desperate effort to save the regimental Colours, for which both were awarded the Victoria Cross. The next day the Zulus attacked the hastily-defended post of Rorke's Drift: two officers and 110 men fought off repeated attacks by 4,000 Zulus, and thus prevented Natal from being overrun. No fewer than eleven Victoria Crosses were won by the gallant defenders at this action.

The 25th Regiment of Foot

THE KING'S OWN SCOTTISH BORDERERS

PRECEDING TITLES

- 1689   The Earl of Leven's Regiment
- 1689   Leven's, or the Edinburgh Regiment (after Killiecrankie)
- 1751   The 25th (Edinburgh) Regiment
- 1782   The 25th (Sussex) Regiment
- 1805   The 25th (The King's Own Borderers) Regiment of Foot
- 1887   The King's Own Scottish Borderers

TODAY

The Regiment is part of the Scottish Division.

        The Botherers
        The Kokky-Olly Birds
        The Kosbees

        'Blue Bonnets over the Border'

THIS famous Regiment was raised at Edinburgh on 19 March 1689 by David Leslie, 3rd Earl of Leven. Its first action was at the Pass of Killiecrankie, and for its distinguished service at this battle the Regiment was awarded the unique privilege of being permitted to gather recruits at any time, without awaiting the leave of the Lord Provost.

The Regiment suffered heavily at Namur (1695), and at Gibraltar (1732) it defended the station against a siege by 20,000 Spanish troops.

The 25th was another 'Minden' regiment, winning a battle honour at this engagement.

In 1793 the 25th Foot was directed to serve as marines, and took part in Lord Howe's sea battle with the French on 1 June 1794.

During the nineteenth century the 25th took part in various campaigns in the Netherlands, Africa, Canada, the Afghan Wars, India, and many other places.

The 26th Regiment of Foot

THE CAMERONIANS (SCOTTISH RIFLES)

PRECEDING TITLES
    1689   The Cameronians
    1751   The 26th Regiment of Foot
    1786   The 26th, The Cameronians
    1881   The Cameronians (Scottish Rifles)

The Regiment was to have formed part of the Lowland Brigade of the Scottish Division, but was disbanded in 1968.

NICKNAME
(None recorded)

REGIMENTAL MARCH
'Within a Mile of Edinburgh Town'

THE 26th Regiment of Foot was raised in April 1689, the first Colonel being the young Earl of Angus, a member of the Douglas family.

The Regiment served under Marlborough in Flanders, winning battle honours at Bleinheim, Ramillies, Oudenarde, and other engagements. It fought with great distinction with Abercromby in Egypt, and gained further battle honours in Spain and China.

In 1881 the 26th Foot was designated a Rifle Regiment. After some 280 years of honourable and distinguished service, at its own request it was disbanded on 14 May 1968, just about half a mile from the spot where it was originally raised.

The origin of this famous Regiment is of considerable interest. The men first recruited were drawn chiefly from the Cameronian Sect, who were followers of the young Scottish religious reformer, Richard Cameron. Cameron led a small but zealous group of Presbyterians (called Covenanters) whose object was to combat religious intolerance and to preserve the Presbyterian Church in Scotland.

Recruits to the Regiment were always issued with a Bible as a tribute to the memory of the Regiment's religious origin. Even in modern times their religious services were traditionally held out-of-doors, and armed picquets were posted to give the 'all-clear' before the service began.

THE ROYAL INNISKILLING FUSILIERS

PRECEDING TITLES
>   1689   Tiffin's Regiment of Foot
>   1751   The 27th (Enniskilling) Regiment of Foot
>   1881   The Royal Inniskilling Fusiliers

TODAY
>   On 1 July 1968 the Regiment merged with The Royal Ulster Rifles and The Royal Irish Fusiliers (Princess Victoria's) to form The Royal Irish Rangers, a 'large' regiment of the King's Division.

NICKNAMES
>>   The Skins
>>   The Lumps
>>   Skillingers

REGIMENTAL MARCHES
>>   'The British Grenadiers'
>>   'Sprig of Shillelagh'

WILLIAM III raised the 27th Regiment of Foot in 1689, recruiting many men from the defenders of Enniskillen when that town was attacked by the army of James II; the badge of the Castle of Enniskilling was awarded to the Regiment in 1691. The spelling was changed to 'Inniskilling' in 1840.

The 27th Foot gave splendid service in the West Indies, winning the battle honours 'Martinique' (1762), 'Havannah' and 'St Lucia'.

They fought with great distinction in the Peninsular War and at Waterloo, where it is said that Wellington pointed to the Inniskillings, saying 'That is the Regiment that saved the centre of my line'.

Their nickname, 'the Skins', is an obvious abbreviation of 'Inniskilling'. An apocryphal story has it that after the Battle of Maida (1806) the 27th was taking a refreshing dip in the sea when an alarm was given of an impending enemy attack—the troops seized their weapons and paraded 'starkers': hence 'the Skins'.

The Inniskillings are the only Irish regiment to use the Brian Boru bagpipes, which have a keyed chanter and a greater range of notes than the Scottish pipes.

The 28th Regiment of Foot

THE GLOUCESTERSHIRE REGIMENT

PRECEDING TITLES
- 1694 Gibson's Regiment of Foot
- 1751 The 28th Regiment of Foot
- 1782 The 28th, North Gloucestershire Regiment
- 1881 The Gloucestershire Regiment

TODAY

The Gloucestershire Regiment has retained its identity and is now a component regiment of the Prince of Wales's Division.

NICKNAMES

The Fore and Afts
The Old Braggs
The Slashers

REGIMENTAL MARCHES

'The Kinncgad Slashers'
'The Highland Piper'

THE Gloucestershire Regiment has a history going back well over 250 years. It was originally raised by Col John Gibson,

Lieutenant-Governor of Portsmouth, in 1694, and became the 28th Regiment in 1751.

The Regiment's history of service includes Newfoundland (1694), Ramillies (1706), the conquest of Canada under Wolfe (1758), the West Indies, and the War of American Independence (1775). The Peninsular War gave the 28th more battle honours – as did the Waterloo campaign, India, and the Crimea.

The Gloucestershire Regiment has the unique distinction of wearing the Sphinx badge at both the back and the front of the head-dress; this commemorates a battle at Alexandria in Egypt (1801) when the 28th Regiment of Foot fought back to back against fierce French attacks on its front and rear.

In 1951 the Gloucesters were cut off by the Chinese on Hill 325 in Korea. For four days, under continuous fire and attack, the Regiment made a heroic stand. Col Carne received the Victoria Cross, and the Regiment received the United States Distinguished Unit Citation and was authorised to wear the citation flash 'The Glorious Gloucesters' on the uniform sleeve.

The nickname 'the Old Braggs' has a direct connection with a former Colonel, Philip Bragg (1734), and 'the Slashers' came from an incident in Canada in 1764 when an unfortunate magistrate had his ear cut off. Rumour had it that the 28th were responsible, but it was never proved.

The 29th Regiment of Foot

THE WORCESTERSHIRE REGIMENT

PRECEDING TITLES

1694   Farrington's Regiment

1698   Disbanded

1702   Farrington's Regiment

1751   The 29th Regiment of Foot

1782   The 29th (Worcestershire) Regiment
1881   The Worcestershire Regiment

TODAY

In 1920 the Regiment linked with The Sherwood Foresters (Nottingham and Derbyshire) Regiment to form The Worcestershire and Sherwood Foresters Regiment, which is a 'large' regiment of the Prince of Wales's Division.

NICKNAMES

The Ever-sworded	Two and a Hook (from
The Vein Openers	the Regiment's number)
Star of the Line	The 'Firms'

REGIMENTAL MARCHES

'Hearts of Oak'	'Royal Windsor'
'Rule Britannia'	'Duchess of Kent'

COL THOMAS FARRINGTON (late of the Coldstream Regiment of Foot Guards) raised the original 29th Foot on 16 February 1694. It was disbanded for a time four years later, but raised again in 1702 with the same officers as before – they had been on half pay in the meantime.

The 29th Regiment of Foot fought in Flanders under Marlborough (1706), winning as their first battle honour 'Ramillies'. They then saw action in the Americas, and served as marines under Lord Howe (1794). The Peninsular War (1808–13) saw the Regiment gaining further well-deserved battle honours.

After service in the West Indies (1840) the Regiment fought with great distinction in the Sikh Wars (1845–58).

The nicknames of this Regiment, having historical links, are of considerable interest. 'Ever-sworded' arises from an incident one night in September 1746 when, while the officers of the Regiment were at mess in their station in North America, they were treacherously attacked by Red Indians who were believed to be loyal. The attack was

44

beaten off, but to guard against similar attacks in the future the custom of wearing swords at mess was instituted.

'The Vein Openers' recalls the part the Regiment played in a regrettable incident known as the Boston Massacre (1770). A detachment of the 29th was forced to open fire on a crowd of colonists – the first spilling of blood which heralded the War of American Independence five years later.

The regimental marches also have historical links. 'Hearts of Oak' and 'Rule Britannia' commemorate marine service. 'Royal Windsor' was given to the Regiment while it was stationed at Windsor (1791) by Princess Augusta, daughter of George III. The regimental slow march 'Duchess of Kent' was composed by Queen Victoria's mother when she herself was Duchess of Kent.

In 1759 Admiral Boscawen brought back from Guadeloupe ten coloured drummer-boys. These he presented to his brother, the then Colonel of the Regiment. The custom of coloured drummers was continued for eighty-four years, the last of them dying in 1843.

The 30th Regiment of Foot

THE EAST LANCASHIRE REGIMENT

PRECEDING TITLES

1694 Lord Castleton's Regiment
1743 Frampton's Regiment
1751 The 30th Regiment of Foot
1782 The 30th, or 1st Cambridge Regiment
1881 The East Lancashire Regiment

TODAY

On 1 July 1958 the Regiment amalgamated with The South Lancashire Regiment, Prince of Wales's Volunteers

(40th Foot) to form The Lancashire Regiment (Prince of Wales's Volunteers). In 1970, a further amalgamation took place with The Loyal Regiment (47th Foot), forming The Queen's Lancashire Regiment (Loyals and Lancashire). This is one of the 'large' regiments of the King's Division.

THE 30th Regiment of Foot was raised by Lord Castleton in 1694, most of the recruits being gathered from Lincolnshire and Yorkshire; in fact, it was not until 1744 that the 30th received its first recruits from Lancashire.

The 30th Foot were one of the six regiments used as marines during the War of the Spanish Succession; the Regiment not only took part in the capture of Gibraltar in 1702, but in the defence of this fortress on many other occasions.

Under Lord Nelson the 30th Foot took part in the siege and capture of Bastia, Corsica. They fought at Badajos, and at Salamanca (1812) they routed a French column, capturing the French Eagle as a regimental trophy.

At Waterloo the 30th Foot formed a square in the front line, and despite fierce action by French gunners and cavalry the square remained unbroken all day. The Regiment paid a heavy price in casualties, however – two-thirds of their officers and men were killed or wounded on that day.

The story goes that at the end of the day Wellington had the 30th Foot moved to a new position. Then the great Duke, looking round, asked his staff 'What is that square lying down?' The answer was 'That is the position from which the 30th have just moved!'

THE EAST SURREY REGIMENT

PRECEDING TITLES

1702   Villier's Marines
1703   Luttrell's Marines
1706   Churchill's Marines
1711   Goring's Marines
1714   The 31st Regiment of Foot
1782   The 31st, Huntingdonshire Regiment
1881   The East Surrey Regiment

TODAY

On 14 October 1959 the Regiment amalgamated with
The Queen's Royal Regiment (West Surrey) to form
The Queen's Royal Surrey Regiment, which is part of
the 'large' Queen's Regiment of the Queen's Division.

NICKNAME

The Young Buffs

REGIMENTAL MARCHES

'A Southerly Wind and a Cloudy Sky'
'Lord Charles Montague's Huntingdonshire
March' (slow)
'A Life on the Ocean Wave'

THE 31st Regiment of Foot began life as a marine regiment,
and their naval service of over nine years is commemorated
by the inclusion of 'A Life on the Ocean Wave' among the
regimental marches. This tune, as is well known, is the
quick march of the Royal Marines, and in 1949 the Royal
Marines gave permission for the march to be played by the
Regiment. Their hundred years of service as the Huntingdonshire Regiment is of course referred to in the title of their
slow march.

In its early years the 31st had buff facings, and it is said

47

that at Dettingen King George II mistook the 31st for the Buffs (the 3rd Foot): this story is given as the origin of their nickname.

The Regiment has given distinguished service in many campaigns, in particular at Quebec, Fontenoy, and in the Sikh Wars. The 31st Foot was another of the regiments whose officers wore black in their lace in memory of Gen. Wolfe.

The 32nd Regiment of Foot

THE DUKE OF CORNWALL'S LIGHT INFANTRY

PRECEDING TITLES

    1702 Fox's Regiment of Marines
    1715 The 32nd Regiment of Foot
    1782 The 32nd, or Cornwall Regiment
    1858 The 32nd (Cornwall) Light Infantry
    1881 The Duke of Cornwall's Light Infantry

TODAY

On 6 October 1959 the Regiment linked with The Somerset Light Infantry (Prince Albert's) to form The Somerset and Cornwall Light Infantry, which is part of the Light Infantry of the Light Division.

NICKNAMES

    The Docs
    The Surprisers

REGIMENTAL MARCHES

    'Trelawney'
    'One and All'

IN the spring of 1702 Colonel Edward Fox, late of the

King's Holland Regiment, was authorised to raise a regiment of marines. This was later to become the 32nd Foot. Its first service was under Admiral Sir George Rooke at Cadiz and Vigo (1702), followed by Gibraltar (1704-5). The 32nd Regiment then fought at Dettingen (1743) and Fontenoy (1745) in the War of the Austrian Succession.

In the Napoleonic Wars (1803-15) the 32nd fought with distinction, winning battle honours at Corunna, Salamanca, Quatre Bras, and Waterloo.

Then, after service in Canada (1830-41), came departure for India where the Regiment fought in the Second Sikh War. One of the outstanding actions in which it was involved was the defence of the Residency at Lucknow during the Indian Mutiny (1857). The siege itself lasted for the best part of five months, and for three of these months the 32nd was the sole defender. For this gallant service the Regiment was honoured by being granted Light Infantry status (1858).

Prior to 1933 the Regiment had the two regimental marches shown. However, as official sanction only allowed them one march, the two were combined and retained the title 'One and All'.

The 33rd Regiment of Foot

THE DUKE OF WELLINGTON'S REGIMENT (WEST RIDING)

PRECEDING TITLES

1702   Huntingdon's Regiment of Foot
1747   (ranked as the 33rd Regiment)
1751   The 33rd Regiment of Foot
1782   The 33rd (The 1st Yorkshire West Riding) Regiment of Foot

1853   The 33rd (The Duke of Wellington's) Regiment
         of Foot
1881   The Duke of Wellington's Regiment (West
         Riding)

TODAY
The Regiment is now one of the regiments of the King's
Division.

NICKNAMES
>   The Havercake Lads
>   The Dukes

REGIMENTAL MARCHES
>   'The Wellesley'
>   'Ilkla Moor'
>   'I'm Ninety-five'

THE FIRST DUKE OF WELLINGTON, Arthur Wellesley,
had a long association with the 33rd Regiment of Foot. In
his early years he was on the strength of the 76th Foot (the
Regiment which later became the 2nd Battalion of the 33rd
Foot). Later, in April 1793, the future Duke was a Major
with the 33rd Foot, and as Lieutenant-Colonel he assumed
command of this Regiment on 30 September of the same
year. This was, in fact, Wellington's first command, and it
was during this period that he became the victor of the
Peninsula. He was Colonel of the Regiment from 1807 to
1813.

After Wellington's death in 1852, Queen Victoria granted
the Regiment the secondary title 'The Duke of Wellington's'
in honour of the great Duke (*London Gazette*, 28 June 1853).

The present form of title of the Regiment was adopted
on 1 January 1921. It is the only regiment in the British
Army named after a person not of royal blood. In addition
it is the only regiment to have scarlet facings.

Wellington's crest is part of the Regiment's badge. The ancient nickname 'Havercake Lads' is said to originate from the eighteenth-century practice of recruiting sergeants who carried oatcakes on their sword points when drumming for recruits.

The 34th Regiment of Foot

THE BORDER REGIMENT

PRECEDING TITLES

1702   Lucas's Regiment

1751   The 34th Regiment of Foot

1782   The 34th, or Cumberland Regiment

1881   The Border Regiment

TODAY

In October 1959 the Regiment linked with The King's Own Royal Regiment (Lancaster) to form The King's Own Royal Border Regiment, which is a 'large' regiment of the King's Division.

NICKNAME

The Cattle Reevers

REGIMENTAL MARCHES

'D'ye ken John Peel'

'March of the French 34ième Regiment de Ligne'

THIS famous Regiment was raised on 12 February 1702 – one of several new regiments embodied when Louis XIV of France made his grandson King of Spain.

The 34th Foot saw active service in Flanders and Spain (1705–13), following this by service at Gibraltar during the siege (1727), and a period of service as marines in 1740.

During the Peninsular War it was in the thick of most of the fighting (1809–14), but one particular battle merits special mention. On 28 October 1811 at Arroyo dos Molinos the Regiment captured a battalion of the French 34ieme Regiment, including the band and drums.

The anniversary of the battle is still celebrated annually by the Regiment parading the captured drums. The Border Regiment is the only regiment to bear 'Arroyo dos Molinos' as a battle honour.

During World War II the Border Regiment, as part of the 1st Airborne Division, was the first British unit to enter a major action by glider. The action was the invasion of Sicily in 1943.

The Regiment's nickname is said to come from the days when cattle rustlers used to cross the Scottish border, in both directions. The name is, however, very seldom used today.

The 35th Regiment of Foot

THE ROYAL SUSSEX REGIMENT

PRECEDING TITLES

    1701   Lord Donegall's Regiment
    1751   The 35th Regiment of Foot
    1782   The 35th, or Dorsetshire Regiment
    1804   The 35th, or Sussex Regiment
    1832   The 35th (Royal Sussex) Regiment
    1881   The Royal Sussex Regiment

TODAY

In December 1966 the Regiment became a component

unit of the 'large' Queen's Regiment of the Queen's Division.

NICKNAMES
The Belfast Regiment
The Orange Lillies

REGIMENTAL MARCHES
'Royal Sussex'
'Rousillon'

ARTHUR CHICHESTER, 3RD EARL OF DONEGALL, raised this Regiment in 1701. It was named the 35th, or Dorsetshire Regiment in 1782, but in 1804 Charles Lennox (later Duke of Richmond), who was then Colonel of the Regiment, recruited many Sussex men and persuaded the Army authorities to change the name to the Sussex Regiment, a title at that time held by the 25th Regiment of Foot. (It was this same Duke of Richmond who gave the famous 'eve of battle' ball before Waterloo.) Col Lennox was eventually invested with the Order of the Garter, which is possibly why the Star of that Order appears in the regimental badge.

Before this the Regiment fought at Gibraltar (1704–5), at Barcelona under the Earl of Peterborough, and in several other famous engagements. In 1759, under Wolfe at Quebec, it defeated the famous French regiment the Royal Rousillon, and after the battle the men of the 35th 'picked up the white plumes as worn by the French and stuck them in their own hats'. The wearing of the Rousillon plume, abolished in 1810, was restored in 1901. The nickname 'Orange Lillies' may have arisen from the Regiment's orange facings, authorised by William III in 1701; Lord Donegall was an 'Orangeman'. Alternatively, the name may be linked with the capture of the Royal Rousillon Colours, which carried the fleur-de-lis. When the 34th became a 'Royal' regiment in 1832, the facing colour was changed to blue.

THE WORCESTERSHIRE REGIMENT – 2ND BATTALION

PRECEDING TITLES

 1702   Charlemont's Regiment
 1751   The 36th Regiment of Foot
 1782   The 36th (Herefordshire) Regiment
 1881   2nd Battalion, The Worcestershire Regiment

TODAY
 See The 29th Regiment of Foot.

NICKNAME
 The Saucy Greens

REGIMENTAL MARCH
 'The Lincolnshire Poacher'

In 1701 William IV commissioned William Caulfield, 2nd Viscount Charlemont, to raise a regiment of foot. Charlemont's Regiment was raised in Ireland and was originally intended for marine service; after taking part in a naval expedition to Cadiz, the Regiment was ordered to the West Indies (1703), and followed this by service in Spain (1705) under Charles Mordaunt, Earl of Peterborough.

Next came action in India, assisting The Honourable East India Company against Haidar Ali, Sultan of Mysore, and his son Tippoo (1783–92). King William IV granted the 36th Foot the honour 'Hindoostan' for its outstanding service in India.

The 36th was at Rolica in the Peninsular War and received special commendation from Wellesley in his dispatches. It was also with Sir John Moore at Corunna (1809), earning the battle honour of that name.

It is said that the motto 'Firm', borne on the badge and

Colours of The Worcestershire Regiment, was originally granted to the 36th Foot as a testimony to its long record of heroic and loyal service.

Because of its Irish origin the 36th had grass-green facings, and this colour, together with an alleged fondness for the fair sex, earned the Regiment its nickname 'Saucy Greens'.

The regimental march marks the Regiment's traditional friendship and long association with the 10th Foot (the old Lincolnshire Regiment), with which it shared many campaigns.

The 37th Regiment of Foot

THE ROYAL HAMPSHIRE REGIMENT

PRECEDING TITLES
- 1702   Meredith's Regiment
- 1751   The 37th Regiment of Foot
- 1782   The 37th, or North Hampshire Regiment
- 1881   The Hampshire Regiment
- 1946   The Royal Hampshire Regiment

TODAY

The Regiment has retained its identity and is now a component regiment of the Prince of Wales's Division.

NICKNAME

The Tigers

REGIMENTAL MARCHES

'The Highland Piper'
'The Farmer's Boy'
'The Hampshires'

ON 13 February 1702 Thomas Meredith, the then Adjutant-

General, was commissioned to raise a regiment of foot, which in 1751 was officially numbered and given precedence as the 37th Regiment of Foot.

The Regiment's splendid record of service includes the War of the Spanish Succession, the Seven Years' War (1756), War of American Independence, the Peninsular War, and many other engagements.

The 37th was another of the six 'Minden' regiments which kept up the custom of wearing the Minden Rose on the anniversary of that famous victory. But the rose in the Regiment's badge is said to represent the red Hampshire rose, a badge of Henry V, who awarded it to the City of Winchester in 1415 as he passed through on his way to the Agincourt campaign.

The nickname comes from the Bengal Tiger in the 37th's badge, though this really belongs to the 2nd Battalion (67th Foot). It was awarded to this latter Regiment by George IV to mark distinguished service in India (1805–26).

The 38th Regiment of Foot

THE SOUTH STAFFORDSHIRE REGIMENT

PRECEDING TITLES

- 1705 Lillingston's Regiment of Foot
- 1751 The 38th Regiment of Foot
- 1782 The 38th, or 1st Staffordshire Regiment
- 1881 The South Staffordshire Regiment

TODAY

On 31 January 1959 the Regiment linked with The North Staffordshire Regiment (The Prince of Wales's) to form

The Staffordshire Regiment (The Prince of Wales's), which is a 'large' regiment of the Prince of Wales's Division.

> The Staffordshire Knots
> The Pump and Tortoise Brigade

> 'Over the Hills and Far Away'

COL LUKE LILLINGSTON raised the 38th Foot at the King's Head Hotel in Lichfield in 1705. After a short period of service in Ireland, the Regiment was sent to the West Indies, where it served continuously, both by land and by sea, for fifty-seven years (1707–64). At that time the West Indies was the unhealthiest posting in the British Army.

Grossly neglected, unpaid, and seemingly completely forgotten, the Regiment managed to keep its identity. It was in fact the first Regiment to adopt a form of tropical clothing. This was known as 'holland' fabric (made from sacking used for packing sugar) and was used for lining coats, and making waistcoats and breeches. This long over-seas service was commemorated by King George V in 1936 when the Regiment was granted the distinction of wearing a 'holland' patch behind the badge.

After its West Indies service the 38th served in the Peninsular War (where, unfortunately, all the records were lost), fighting with outstanding distinction at Corunna, Salamanca, Burgos, and San Sebastian. The War of American Independence saw the Regiment at Bunker's Hill and Brandywine, and it fought in the Crimea at Alma, Inkerman, and Sevastopol, following this by sterling service in India during the Mutiny (1857), including a part in the Relief of Lucknow.

The Stafford knot in the badge of the Regiment is thought to be the ancient device of the Stafford family. The

38th wore this knot as a cap badge from 1870, but before that it was worn on the skirt turn-back of the old scarlet coat.

The 39th Regiment of Foot

THE DORSET REGIMENT

TODAY

On 17 May 1958 the Regiment linked with The Devonshire Regiment to form The Devonshire and Dorset Regiment which is a 'large' regiment of the Prince of Wales's Division.

NICKNAMES

Sankey's Horse
The Green Linnets

REGIMENTAL MARCHES

'The Maid of Glenconnel'
'The Farmer's Boy'
'The Dorsetshire'

THE 39th Regiment of Foot was raised in Ireland by Col Richard Coote, who was later killed in a duel. The Regiment was then taken over by Col (later Lt-Gen.) Sankey. This famous Regiment was the first Crown Infantry

Regiment to serve in active operation in India: it served under Robert Clive at his great victory, Plassey (23 June 1757). Recognition of this service was given by the official granting of the motto *Primus in India*, together with the battle honour 'Plassey', a unique award in the British Army. The Dorsets are the proud owners of a silver-headed Drum Major's staff, presented to the Regiment by the Nawab of Arcot, in memory of Plassey.

The Castle and Key in the Dorsets' badge marks their part in the defence of Gibraltar during the great siege of 1779–83. They were, in fact, the only regiment present at the siege that had also defended Gibraltar in 1726–7.

In the Peninsular War the 39th Regiment of Foot distinguished itself at Badajos, Albuera, and Vittoria (1811–13).

The nickname 'Sankey's Horse' arose from the fact that the Regiment was mounted on mules during the march to Almanza (23 April 1707); the 'Green Linnets' was a mid-eighteenth-century name given to the 39th because of its green facings.

The 40th Regiment of Foot

THE SOUTH LANCASHIRE REGIMENT (THE PRINCE OF WALES'S VOLUNTEERS)

PRECEDING TITLES

1717	Philip's Regiment
1751	The 40th Regiment of Foot
1782	The 40th, or 2nd Somersetshire Regiment
1881	The South Lancashire Regiment (The Prince of Wales's Volunteers)

On 1 July 1958 the Regiment linked with The East Lancashire Regiment to form The Lancashire Regiment (Prince of Wales's Volunteers). On 27 March 1970 a further amalgamation with The Loyal Regiment (North Lancashire) took place and formed The Queen's Lancashire Regiment (Loyals and Lancashire), which is a 'large' regiment of the King's Division.

NICKNAMES

The Excellers
The Fighting 40th

REGIMENTAL MARCHES

'God Bless the Prince of Wales'
'The Lancashire Witches'
'The South Lancashire Regiment'

IN 1717, the first year of the reign of George I, the 40th Regiment of Foot was raised on a permanent basis. At the time there were four independent companies of foot stationed at Annapolis Royal (the then name of the new settlement in Nova Scotia) and four other independent companies based at Placentia on the island of Newfoundland. It was from these units that the Regiment was raised. Right up to the beginning of the nineteenth century the 40th Foot served solely in various parts of the American continent.

Later the Regiment saw service in Egypt, and its distinction in action was acknowledged by the granting of the Sphinx as a regimental badge; it is said that the nickname 'the Fighting 40th' arose from excellent service in the Egyptian campaign.

The other nickname, 'Excellers', is derived from the roman form of the regimental number XL.

Until 1881 the Regiment does not appear to have had any Lancashire connections – it was in fact the 2nd Somersetshire Regiment in 1782.

The 41st Regiment of Foot

THE WELCH REGIMENT

TODAY

On 11 June 1969 the Regiment linked with The South Wales Borderers to form The Royal Regiment of Wales, a 'large' regiment of the Prince of Wales's Division.

NICKNAMES

The Invalids
Wardour's Horse

REGIMENTAL MARCH

'Ap Shenkin'

ON 11 March 1719 a Royal Warrant was issued authorising the raising of a regiment of 'invalids', to be known as the 41st Regiment of Foot. The Regiment was to be recruited mainly from pensioners and men who, though willing to serve in the Regular Army, were not considered fit for such service, either because of disablement or other physical disability. It could be used for garrison duty, or in an emergency could be called upon to aid the civil authorities in the keeping of the peace. It was known as the Invalids Regiment, and although the facings were blue, it cannot be established that this was ever a Royal regiment.

In 1787 the decision was taken to bring the Regiment into line with other Army units. The rank and file were retired and pensioned off, and their places taken by officers and men seconded from other regiments.

61

The record of active service includes distinguished action in America (1812–13). The Regiment fought in Afghanistan and in the Crimea, giving outstanding service at Alma, Inkerman, and Sevastopol.

The 41st was not granted a regional title until 1831; later, with the Cardwell Reforms of 1881, the official title became 'The Welsh Regiment'. The revised spelling 'Welch' was adopted in 1920 (Army Order 56 of 1920).

The 42nd Regiment of Foot
THE BLACK WATCH
(ROYAL HIGHLAND REGIMENT)

PRECEDING TITLES

1725 to 1739	Independent Companies – *Am Freiceadan Dubh*, or The Black Watch
1739	The Highland Regiment of Foot
1751	The 42nd Regiment of Foot
1758	The 42nd (The Royal Highland) Regiment of Foot
1861	The 42nd (The Royal Highland) Regiment, The Black Watch
1881	The Black Watch (Royal Highlanders)
1934	The Black Watch (Royal Highland Regiment)

TODAY

The Black Watch is a component regiment of the Scottish Division.

NICKNAME

The Forty Twa

REGIMENTAL MARCHES

'Highland Laddie'

'Blue Bonnets over the Border'

THIS famous Regiment can trace its origin back to the

Independent Companies of Highlanders who had policed their wild homeland since 1725. King George II authorised the combining of these Companies into a regiment in 1739, and the first Colonel was Sir Robert Munro of Foulis. The dark tartan gave rise to the name 'Black Watch' and this is the only item of the regimental dress that has remained unchanged to this day.

The 42nd Regiment has a long record of distinguished service over the many years of its existence: Fontenoy in 1745, the Seven Years' War, America, Canada, Egypt, the Peninsular War and the Waterloo campaign, the Crimea, the Indian Mutiny (where the Regiment gained no fewer than eight V.C.s), the Nile Expedition, the South African War, and the two World Wars.

The Regiment was given the honour of a 'Royal' title in 1758 – a just reward for what was described at the time as 'their extraordinary courage, loyalty and exemplary conduct'.

The Black Watch boasts a legendary character in Donald Macleod of Skye, formerly a sergeant in the Royal Scots. In 1740 he resigned from the Royal Scots to join this new Highland Regiment, and in all served seventy-five years with the Black Watch, retiring at the age of 103 to settle in London. At that time his eldest son was eighty-three and his youngest son nine years old!

The 43rd Regiment of Foot
THE OXFORDSHIRE AND BUCKING-HAMSHIRE LIGHT INFANTRY

PRECEDING TITLES

1741 Fowle's Regiment of Foot
1747 The 54th Regiment of Foot
1751 The 43rd Regiment of Foot
1782 The 43rd (Monmouth) Regiment of Foot

1803   The 43rd (Monmouthshire) Regiment of Foot,
       Light Infantry
1881   The Oxfordshire Light Infantry
1908   The Oxfordshire and Buckinghamshire Light
       Infantry

TODAY

In 1966 the Regiment became the 1st Battalion, The
Royal Green Jackets. In 1968 it was completely absorbed
in this new 'large' regiment, which is a component of
the Light Division.

NICKNAMES

Wolfe's Own
Light Brigade

REGIMENTAL MARCHES

'Das Nach Lager von Grenada'
'The Italian Song'

THE 43rd Regiment of Foot was raised in 1741 as Fowle's
Regiment of Foot; it soon came to be connected with the
County of Monmouthshire, and in 1803 was one of the
first regiments of the British Army to be selected by Sir
John Moore for special training for conversion to Light
Infantry.

The record of service includes the action leading to the
capture of Quebec under Gen. Wolfe (1759), and the
Battle of Bunker's Hill (1759).

The 43rd Regiment, as part of the Light Division, fought
with outstanding distinction throughout the Peninsular
War, earning many battle honours and a special commendation from the military historian Napier.

A number of troops of the 43rd Regiment were among
those heroic men who sacrificed their lives to save women
and children when the *Birkenhead* was wrecked.

A final point of interest: this Regiment is the only one
in which the officers wear a white tie with mess kit.

THE ESSEX REGIMENT

PRECEDING TITLES

1741 Long's Regiment of Foot
1751 The 44th Regiment of Foot
1782 The 44th, East Essex Regiment
1881 The Essex Regiment

TODAY

In 1958 the Regiment amalgamated with The Bedford-shire and Hertfordshire Regiment to form The 3rd East Anglian Regiment; and in 1964 all the East Anglian regiments were linked to form The Royal Anglian Regiment of the Queen's Division. This was the first 'large' regiment of the British Army.

NICKNAMES

The Two Fours
The Little Fighting Fours

REGIMENTAL MARCHES

'The Hampshires'
'Rule Britannia'
'The Essex'

THE 44th Regiment of Foot was raised during the War of the Austrian Succession (1741) by Col James Long, late of the 1st (Grenadier) Guards.

In 1745 the Regiment fought at Prestonpans, and then had ten years of severe campaigning in North America. It was again in America for the War of American Independence in 1775, and followed this with six years in Canada (1780–6).

The Regiment served with great distinction under Wellington during the Peninsular War: it was at Salamanca

(1812) that Lt W. Pearce of the 44th Regiment captured the Eagle Standard of the French 62nd Infantry Regiment. This feat of arms was commemorated by the adoption of the Eagle as the regimental crest.

The 44th was at Waterloo, and also in the Crimea, where it gained the battle honours 'Alma', 'Inkerman', and 'Sevastopol'. During the Afghan War of 1841 the 44th Regiment of Foot was part of that unfortunate British garrison which was annihilated while attempting to retire from Kabul to Jellalabad: the final stand was by twenty men of the 44th Foot at Gundamuk, and there Lt Souter, at great risk to his own life, eventually saved the regimental Colour.

The nicknames, of course, originate from the regimental number. 'Rule Britannia' is played as a regimental march to commemorate service as a marine regiment in the West Indies (1789–1802).

The 45th Regiment of Foot

THE SHERWOOD FORESTERS (NOTTINGHAM AND DERBYSHIRE) REGIMENT

PRECEDING TITLES

66

1902 **The Sherwood Foresters (Nottingham and Derbyshire) Regiment**

In 1970 the Regiment amalgamated with The Worcestershire Regiment to form The Worcestershire and Sherwood Foresters Regiment, a 'large' regiment of the Prince of Wales's Division.

NICKNAMES

The Old Stubborns
The Hosiers
The Green Marines

REGIMENTAL MARCH

'The Young May Moon'

THE first 45th Regiment, raised as marines, was actually disbanded in 1748, but in 1741 Col Houghton raised the regiment later to become the 45th Foot.

This famous Regiment served some twenty of its early years in Canada, winning battle honours against the French (Louisburg), and followed this by many engagements against the Americans in the War of American Independence (1776).

It was during the Peninsular War that the 45th Foot earned the nickname 'the Old Stubborns' at the Battle of Talavera (1809). This was, of course, only one of the many honours gained by its conspicuous bravery in many battles, among which are numbered Busaco, Salamanca, and Vittoria.

After service in Ceylon, the 45th fought in the Burmese War (1824–5), the Kaffir War in South Africa, and the Abyssinian campaign of 1867 under Lord Napier.

A romantic little story relates the stag and oak-leaves in the Regiment's badge to the wooded areas of Nottinghamshire and Derbyshire, and the green facings of the Regiment to Robin Hood, who used this 'camouflage' in Sherwood

67

Forest. But the original 45th had green facings (hence the nickname 'the Green Marines') long before Robin Hood had become the respectable character he is today.

The regimental march of the 45th Foot was a tune taken from the comic opera *Robin Hood*, of about the year 1784.

The 46th Regiment of Foot

THE DUKE OF CORNWALL'S LIGHT INFANTRY – 2ND BATTALION

PRECEDING TITLES

- 1741   Price's, 57th Regiment of Foot
- 1748   The 46th Regiment of Foot
- 1782   The 46th (South Devon) Regiment
- 1881   2nd Battalion, the Duke of Cornwall's Light Infantry

TODAY

See The 32nd Regiment of Foot.

NICKNAMES

Murrey's Bucks	The Edinburgh Regiment
The Red Feathers	The Lacedemonians

REGIMENTAL MARCH

'One and All'

WITH the threat of the outbreak of war in Europe in 1741, the usual eleventh hour steps were taken to increase the English Army Establishment, one of the new regiments to be raised being Col Price's 57th Regiment of Foot.

The first action was at Prestonpans (1745) against the Young Pretender. Later, after being re-numbered as the

46th, the Regiment fought against the French in Canada at Ticonderoga and Niagara (1758–9).

In the War of American Independence (1776–82) the 46th Regiment inflicted a humiliating defeat on the Americans at Brandywine Creek: the Americans were known to have vowed vengeance, and so, to assist in identification, the men of the 46th wore red feathers in their head-gear, making sure that the Americans were fully aware of this badge.

The nicknames are of interest: 'Murrey's Bucks' was derived from the name of the Colonel in 1745. The origin of 'the Edinburgh Regiment' cannot be traced, but 'the Lacedemonians' is said to have arisen from an incident when, while under fire, the Commanding Officer of the the 46th lectured his men on the discipline of the Lacedemonians.

The 47th Regiment of Foot

THE LOYAL REGIMENT (NORTH LANCASHIRE)

PRECEDING TITLES

- 1741 Mordaunt's Regiment
- 1748 The 47th Regiment of Foot
- 1782 The 47th (Lancashire) Regiment
- 1881 The Loyal North Lancashire Regiment
- 1921 The Loyal Regiment (North Lancashire)

TODAY

On 27 March 1970 the Regiment linked with The Lancashire Regiment (Prince of Wales's Volunteers) to form The Queen's Lancashire Regiment (Loyals and Lancashire), which is a 'large' regiment of the King's Division.

NICKNAMES

The Cauliflowers
The Lancashire Lads
Wolfe's Own

REGIMENTAL MARCHES

'The Red, Red Rose'
'The Mountain Rose'

COL JOHN MORDAUNT raised this Regiment on 3 January 1741. A previous 47th, a marine regiment, had been disbanded – one of six marine regiments (44th to 49th) all disbanded round about 1748. These, when they were raised again in 1755, were placed under direct Admiralty control, becoming the Royal Marines of today.

The record of service of the 47th Regiment of Foot includes the Battle of Prestonpans (1745), followed by service in Canada under Wolfe at Quebec (1759), where the Regiment's outstanding performance earned it the nickname 'Wolfe's Own'. The Regiment wore a black line in the gold lace of the uniform as an expression of sorrow at Wolfe's death. To this day the black line is still evident, as is the black lanyard worn by officers and warrant officers.

The 47th fought in the War of American Independence, the Peninsular War, and India (1806). After Gibraltar, Malta, and the West Indies it fought with great distinction in the Crimean War (1854), where its first V.C. was won at Inkerman.

The rose in the regimental badge is of course the red rose of Lancashire, adopted in 1782. The nickname 'Cauliflowers' is said to originate from the white facings, white being quite uncommon as a facing colour.

The 48th Regiment of Foot

THE NORTHAMPTONSHIRE
REGIMENT

TODAY

In June 1960 the Regiment linked with The Royal Lincolnshire Regiment to form The 2nd East Anglian Regiment (Duchess of Gloucester's Own Royal Lincolnshire and Northamptonshire). Later, in 1968, the County affiliations were dropped and the Regiment was totally absorbed in The Royal Anglian Regiment, which is a 'large' regiment of the Queen's Division.

NICKNAME

The Heroes of Talavera

REGIMENTAL MARCHES

'The Northamptonshire'
'The Lincolnshire Poacher'

THE War of the Austrian Succession necessitated an increase in the English standing army, and as a result instructions were issued for the raising of seven new regiments.

On 17 January 1741, Col the Hon. James Cholmondeley was commissioned to raise a regiment of foot – this he did, the Regiment being embodied at Norwich. At the time of the Regiment's formation it was given precedence as the 59th Regiment of the Line. But in 1748 there was a reduction in the number of marine regiments, and in consequence the 59th was renumbered '48th'.

The Regiment fought with distinction at Quebec under Gen. Wolfe (1759). In fact, after the Cardwell Reforms of 1881, the Northamptonshire Regiment was the only remaining unit to have had *two* battalions at Quebec, the 48th and the 58th.

Among the many battle honours, 'Talavera' (fought on 28 July 1809) is probably the most noteworthy: after the battle Wellington announced that the 48th Regiment of Foot had saved the day and made victory possible.

The 49th Regiment of Foot

THE ROYAL BERKSHIRE REGIMENT (PRINCESS CHARLOTTE OF WALES'S)

PRECEDING TITLES

- 1744 The 63rd, Trelawney's Regiment of Foot
- 1751 The 49th Regiment of Foot
- 1782 The 49th, or Hertfordshire Regiment
- 1816 The 49th, or Princess of Wales's Hertfordshire Regiment
- 1881 Princess Charlotte of Wales's Berkshire Regiment
- 1885 The Regiment granted the title 'Royal'
- 1921 The Royal Berkshire Regiment (Princess Charlotte of Wales's)

On 9 June 1959 the Regiment linked with The Wiltshire Regiment (Duke of Edinburgh's) to form The Duke of Edinburgh's Royal Regiment (Berkshire and Wiltshire), which is a 'large' regiment of the Prince of Wales's Division.

NICKNAME

The Biscuit Boys

REGIMENTAL MARCHES

'The Dashing White Sergeant'
'The Young May Moon'

THE 49th Regiment of Foot had its origins in eight independent garrison companies in Jamaica. These were amalgamated into a regiment by the Governor, Edward Trelawney, who, although he had no military experience, was appointed the first Colonel. Originally numbered the 63rd, the Regiment was renumbered the 49th Foot in 1751.

The Regiment saw service on the outbreak of the American Rebellion in 1775, and took part in the Brandywine Creek action (1777), earning the right to wear the red Brandywine flash.

Detachments of the 49th Foot served as marines under Sir Hyde Parker (1801) and received the battle honour 'Copenhagen'. The rope coil in the officers' badge is said to commemorate this action, as is the right to play 'Rule, Britannia' after the regimental march.

Princess Charlotte of Wales gave the Regiment her title in 1816, and the China Dragon in the badge marks service in the Chinese 'Opium' War of 1840–3. The 'Royal' title was granted to the Regiment in recognition of its gallant service at Tolfrek in the Sudan in 1885.

The first V.C.s of the Regiment were won by three members of the 49th Foot during the Crimean War.

THE QUEEN'S OWN (ROYAL WEST KENT) REGIMENT

PRECEDING TITLES

1756 The 52nd Regiment of Foot
1757 The 50th Regiment of Foot
1782 The 50th, or West Kent Regiment
1827 The 50th, or the Duke of Clarence's Regiment
1831 The 50th, or the Queen's Own Regiment
1881 The Queen's Own (Royal West Kent) Regiment

TODAY

On 1 March 1961 the Regiment linked with The Buffs (Royal East Kent Regiment) to form The Queen's Own Buffs, Royal Kent Regiment. This latter is a component unit of the 'large' Queen's Regiment of the Queen's Division.

NICKNAMES

The Gallant 50th   The Dirty Half-hundred
The Blind Half-   The Devil's Royals
hundred

REGIMENTAL MARCHES

'A Hundred Pipers'
'Men of Kent'

THERE is a certain amount of confusion about the origins of this Regiment. It is known that in 1741 there was a marine regiment known variously as the 50th Foot or 7th Marines. It had been raised by Maj.-Gen. Cornwall, and was disbanded in 1748. Another false start, under Maj.-Gen. William Shirley, was the raising of another 50th Regiment of Foot in 1754 – to be disbanded in 1755. However, the 52nd Regiment raised by Col James Abercrombie in 1756 was renumbered the 50th Regiment of Foot and continued under that number.

After service at sea with Sir John Mordaunt's expedition to Rochefort (1757), the Regiment campaigned in Ireland, Jamaica, the War of American Independence, Gibraltar, Malta, and Corsica.

It was during service in Egypt (1801) that the Regiment suffered so much from dysentery and ophthalmia that it became known as the 'Blind Half-hundred'.

In the Peninsular War at the battle of Vimeiro (1808) the Regiment became known as the 'Dirty Half-hundred' – not only were the men's faces black from powder, smoke and sweat, but the dye in their black facings ran and added to their discolouration. These facings, so familiar on the battlefields of Portugal and Spain, were changed to blue in 1831 when the 50th became 'The Queen's Own Regiment'.

One of the Regiment's most famous members, Sir Charles Napier, when he had conquered the province of Scinde on the Indian North-West Frontier in 1843, sent to the Governor-General of India the most famous pun in military history: 'Peccavi', which is translated 'I have sinned'.

The 51st Regiment of Foot

THE KING'S OWN YORKSHIRE LIGHT INFANTRY

PRECEDING TITLES

1809   The 51st Light Infantry (Second Yorkshire West Riding)

1821   The 51st King's Own Light Infantry (Second Yorkshire West Riding)

1881   The King's Own Light Infantry (South Yorkshire Regiment)

1887   The King's Own (Yorkshire Light Infantry)

TODAY

On 10 July 1969 the Regiment became part of the Light Infantry 'large' regiment of the Light Division.

NICKNAME

The Koylis

REGIMENTAL MARCHES

'The Jockey of York'
'Jockey to the Fair'

It was Col Robert Napier who raised the 53rd Regiment of Foot in 1755. It was renumbered the 51st and took the name of its new Colonel in 1757.

The 51st Foot played an important part in the Battle of Minden (1759), and after service in Ireland and Minorca, became associated with Sir John Moore, the 'Father' of the Light Infantry, who commanded the Regiment from 1790 to 1795.

Sir John took the 51st to Gibraltar and Corsica. At the Siege of Calvi it was he who was directing the attack when Captain Horatio Nelson, standing beside him, lost the sight of an eye from a stone thrown up by the enemy round shot. Sir John Moore's first commission had been with the 51st, and he was killed at the Battle of Corunna in the year the 51st Foot became the 51st Light Infantry (1809).

After taking part in all Wellington's victories in the Peninsula, the Regiment fought with outstanding distinction at Waterloo.

One tradition dating from Sir John Moore's days is that all Light Infantry regiments march at 140 paces per minute. They carry out drill movements from the 'stand-at-ease' position, and have buglers instead of drummers.

The 52nd Regiment of Foot

THE OXFORDSHIRE AND BUCKINGHAMSHIRE LIGHT INFANTRY – 2ND BATTALION

PRECEDING TITLES

- 1755   The 54th Regiment of Foot
- 1757   The 52nd Regiment of Foot
- 1781   The 52nd (Oxfordshire) Regiment of Foot
- 1803   The 52nd (Oxfordshire) Regiment of Foot, Light Infantry
- 1881   2nd Battalion, The Oxfordshire Light Infantry
- 1908   2nd Battalion, The Oxfordshire and Buckinghamshire Light Infantry

TODAY

See The 43rd Regiment of Foot

NICKNAMES

The Light Bobs
The Light Brigade

REGIMENTAL MARCH

'Lower Castle Yard'

THIS Regiment was raised in 1755 as the 54th Regiment of Foot, and became the 52nd Foot in 1757 – there had been a previous 52nd Regiment, a marine regiment raised in 1742 and disbanded in 1748.

The 52nd was the first regiment to be converted to Light Infantry (1803), and the nickname 'The Light Bobs' is said to stem from this fact; some, however, maintain that its members acquired this nickname owing to their lightheartedness under the most difficult conditions in the Peninsular campaign.

In common with other Light Infantry regiments, the 52nd Foot were lighter equipped than Line infantry, and acted as fast skirmishers, marching at 140 paces per minute.

The 52nd Regiment of Foot has won many battle honours in various campaigns, serving as part of the Light Division. At Waterloo it was the gallant charge of the 52nd Foot that finally broke the resistance of Napoleon's Imperial Guard.

In 1881 the Regiment linked with the 43rd Foot to become a single Regiment.

A custom peculiar to the Oxfordshire and Buckinghamshire Light Infantry was that of never drinking the sovereign's health in the Officers' Mess unless there was present a member of the royal family or a representative of the sovereign.

The 53rd Regiment of Foot

THE KING'S SHROPSHIRE LIGHT INFANTRY

PRECEDING TITLES

1755	The 55th Regiment of Foot
1757	The 53rd Regiment of Foot
1782	The 53rd (Shropshire) Regiment of Foot
1881	The King's Shropshire Light Infantry

In 1968 the Regiment became the 3rd Battalion, the Light Infantry, Light Division.

> The Brickdusts
> The Old Five and Threepennies

> 'Old Towler'
> 'The Farmer's Boy'

COL WILLIAM WHITMORE of Apley, near Bridgnorth in Shropshire, was commissioned to raise a regiment of foot on 21 December 1755. Whitmore's regiment, originally raised as the 55th Regiment, received its final rank as the 53rd in 1757.

The Regiment was stationed at Gibraltar during the Seven Years' War, remaining there until 1768; from time to time it was called upon to do duty as a marine regiment. It next saw action at Quebec and in North America (1776–89), and following this, took part in the war with France (1793–5).

After a period of service in the West Indies, the 53rd (Shropshire) Regiment (as it was now designated) was in India for some years, and then fought with distinction in the Peninsular War, deservedly being awarded several battle honours, including 'Talavera', 'Salamanca', and 'Vittoria'.

In India (1844) the Regiment fought in the Sikh Wars and followed this with fierce engagements during the Indian Mutiny: it was at the Relief of Lucknow (1858) and at Cawnpore, and altogether won four V.C.s in this campaign.

The fact that the 53rd Regiment had red facings was probably what gave rise to the nickname 'Brickdusts'. The other nickname is obviously a play upon the regimental number.

79

THE DORSET REGIMENT –
2ND BATTALION

PRECEDING TITLES

1755   The 56th Regiment of Foot
1757   The 54th Regiment of Foot
1782   The 54th, or West Norfolk Regiment
1831   2nd Battalion, The Dorsetshire Regiment
1951   2nd Battalion, The Dorset Regiment

TODAY

See The 39th Regiment of Foot.

NICKNAME

The Flamers

REGIMENTAL MARCH

'The Dorsetshire'

THE 54th Regiment of Foot was raised in 1755 by Col John Campbell, later fifth Duke of Argyll.

The Sphinx badge and the battle honour 'Marabout' were awarded to the 54th for the service it gave in the Egyptian campaign (1801). It captured Fort Marabout which the French were using to dominate the entrance to Alexandria harbour, and for many years the 54th paraded with one of the captured guns. The award is unique in the British Army: all similar awards are the Sphinx and 'Egypt'.

The Regiment was at Gibraltar in 1802 during a regrettable mutiny by other troops; on this occasion the discipline and loyalty of the 54th earned a special reward presented by the then Duke of Kent – a suitably inscribed silver punch bowl for the Officers' Mess, which is still the centrepiece in the Officer's Mess of the Devonshire and Dorset Regiment.

The nickname 'Flamers' arose from an action by the 54th during the War of American Independence, in the course of which they destroyed by fire many of the enemy ships and buildings at New London.

A very creditable story is told which concerns the Regiment and the troop-ship *Sarah Sands*: while the Regiment was on its way to the Indian Mutiny, fire broke out on board and the panic-stricken crew abandoned ship. But 370 men of the 54th fought and put out the fire, and after a further twelve days of hardship, brought the vessel safely to port on 18 November 1847. Queen Victoria ordered the report of this action to be read to every regiment of the British Army.

The 55th Regiment of Foot

THE BORDER REGIMENT – 2ND BATTALION

PRECEDING TITLES

    1755   The 57th Regiment of Foot
    1757   The 55th Regiment of Foot
    1782   The 55th, Westmoreland Regiment
    1881   The 2nd Battalion, The Border Regiment

TODAY

    See The 34th Regiment of Foot.

NICKNAME

        The Two Fives

REGIMENTAL MARCHES

        'The Lass o' Gowrie'
        'Come back to Erin'

AFTER the raising of the Regiment in 1755, the 55th Foot saw a considerable amount of service in Canada (1757–60) and followed this by arduous campaigning during the War of American Independence. The West Indies was their next scene of operations; then followed tours of duty in Holland, South Africa (the Kaffir Wars), India and Hong Kong.

It was during the 'Opium' War of 1841 that the 55th Regiment captured the only Imperial Dragon Standard taken during the war. For their distinguished service, the 55th Foot was awarded the 'China' dragon to be borne on its Colours.

The Regiment's next major engagements occurred when it was again on active service in the Crimea; Sevastopol, Alma and other major battles were scenes of outstanding bravery by men of the 55th – four men of the Regiment won the Victoria Cross. 'Alma' day (20 September) was always kept as battle honour day by the 55th Regiment of Foot.

The Indian Mutiny and the Burma campaign were also scenes of valiant service by men of the 55th Foot.

The 56th Regiment of Foot

THE ESSEX REGIMENT – 2ND BATTALION

PRECEDING TITLES

See The 44th Regiment of Foot.

Pompadours
The Saucy Pompeys

'Rule, Britannia'

THE 56th Foot (The Essex Regiment) was raised in 1755 by Lord Charles Manners, son of the Duke of Rutland. There had been an earlier 56th Regiment of Foot raised in 1741 and renumbered the 45th Foot in 1751, ultimately becoming the Sherwood Foresters.

The 56th first saw action in Cuba (1762), and followed this by twelve years at Gibraltar, which service included the Great Siege (1779–83).

After a campaign in the West Indies (1793–9) there followed the Napoleonic War, when many Irishmen were recruited into the ranks of the 'Pompadours', as the 56th were now called. The gallant service of these Irishmen is still commemorated on St Patrick's Day (17 March) by the custom of the Corps of Drums beating reveille, and the playing of traditional Irish airs.

The nickname 'Pompadours' has an amusing origin: the Regiment's crimson facings (1764) were not considered a satisfactory colour, and it was decided to change to blue, but this change was not allowed as this was not a royal regiment. So a compromise was settled upon – rose-purple, the favourite colour of the Marquise de Pompadour, *chère-amie* of Louis XV of France.

The playing of 'Rule, Britannia' as a regimental march commemorates the Regiment's service as marine troops in the West Indies.

THE MIDDLESEX REGIMENT
(DUKE OF CAMBRIDGE'S OWN)

PRECEDING TITLES

 1755 The 59th Regiment of Foot
 1757 The 57th Regiment of Foot
 1782 The 57th (West Middlesex) Regiment of Foot
 1881 The Middlesex Regiment (Duke of Cambridge's
    Own)

TODAY

 The Regiment is now part of the 'large' Queen's
 Regiment of the Queen's Division.

NICKNAMES

  The Die-hards
  The Steelbacks
  The Fighting Villains

REGIMENTAL MARCHES

  'Sir Manley Power'
  'Daughter of the Regiment' (slow)
  'Lass o' Gowrie'

THE Regiment's many battle honours include famous actions in the Crimean and Peninsular campaigns. One of the most notable of these, during the Peninsular War, gave rise to the celebrated nickname of the 57th Foot, 'The Die-hards'.

At the battle of Albuera (16 May 1811) the 57th had already lost 428 men of the strength of 647 when their C.O., Col Inglis, was fatally wounded. But he would not allow himself to be carried off the field. Instead, he insisted on being placed near the Colours, from which position he called out to his men, 'Die hard, the 57th, die hard!'

The last survivor of this action, Henry Holloway,

bequeathed to the Regiment his medal with five bars. It is now incorporated in a loving cup, which on Albuera Day is taken from the Officers' Mess to the Sergeants' Mess, where a toast is drunk to the memory of those who fell at Albuera.

The 'Steelbacks' nickname is said to arise from the nume ous floggings earned and endured by the men when the Regiment was at Gibraltar in 1800; this particular nickname is not confined exclusively to the 57th!

The 58th Regiment of Foot

THE NORTHAMPTONSHIRE REGIMENT – 2ND BATTALION

PRECEDING TITLES
1755   The 60th Regiment of Foot
1757   The 58th Regiment of Foot
1782   The 58th, Rutlandshire Regiment
1881   2nd Battalion, The Northamptonshire Regiment

TODAY
See The 48th Regiment of Foot.

NICKNAMES
The Black Cuffs
The Steelbacks

REGIMENTAL MARCH
'The Lincolnshire Poacher'

IN 1755 the requirements of the Seven Years' War necessitated an increase in the strength of the army: it was decided to raise eleven additional regiments of foot.

As a result, on 28 December 1755 Col Robert Anstruther (late Lieutenant-Colonel of the 26th Regiment of Foot, The Cameronians) was commissioned to raise a regiment

85

which was given the number '60' in the order of precedence. In 1757, by reason of the disbanding of the 50th and 51st Regiments, the 60th Foot were raised in rank to become the 58th Regiment of the Line.

The 58th Foot was one of the five regiments which served as garrison troops during the Siege of Gibraltar (1779–83); for this, the Regiment was granted the Castle and Key device for a cap badge, and the battle honour 'Gibraltar'.

The Regiment fought under Gen. Wolfe at Quebec (1759), and gave distinguished service at Alexandria (1801); for this latter action it wears the Sphinx as an embellishment on buttons and badges. Other famous actions involving the 58th were Salamanca and Burgos (1812) in the Peninsular War.

Another distinction of the 58th is the fact that it was the last British regiment to carry its Colours into action: this was at Laing's Nek in the first Boer War, on 28 January 1881.

As to the nicknames, 'Black Cuffs' arose from the black regimental facings, while the other nickname came from the men's apparent complete indifference to and contempt of floggings as a punishment.

The 59th Regiment of Foot

THE EAST LANCASHIRE REGIMENT – 2ND BATTALION

PRECEDING TITLES

See the 30th Regiment of Foot.

The Lilywhites

'The Lancashire Lad'

COL CHARLES MONTAGUE of Nottingham raised what was to be the 59th Regiment of Foot in December 1755.

There seem to have been an extraordinary number of alterations to the designated number of the 59th – at various times the Regiment was the 48th, the 56th, and the 61st. It was even The West Lancashire for a short time in 1881.

The 59th fought with outstanding distinction at Bunker's Hill (1755), at St Vincent, Malta, and Corunna: at this latter action it covered itself with glory by a brilliant bayonet charge.

At the recapture of the Cape of Good Hope (1805), the 59th Foot fought under the command of Sir David Baird. In 1857 the 59th was the sole English regiment serving at the capture of Canton, and it holds this battle honour as a unique distinction.

The 59th Foot, like the 56th Foot, originally had crimson facings, and afterwards changed them to purple.

The 60th Regiment of Foot

THE KING'S ROYAL RIFLE CORPS

PRECEDING TITLES
1755   The 62nd (Royal American) Regiment of Foot
1757   The 60th (Royal American) Regiment of Foot
1824   The 60th (The Duke of York's Rifle Corps and
(June)   Light Infantry) Regiment

1824 The 60th (The Duke of York's Own Rifle Corps)
(July) Regiment
1830 The 60th (The King's Royal Rifle Corps) Regiment
1881 The King's Royal Rifle Corps

TODAY

In 1966 the Regiment became the 2nd Battalion, The Royal Green Jackets. In 1968 it was completely absorbed into that new 'large' regiment, which is a component of the Light Division.

NICKNAMES

The Green Jackets	The 60th Rifles
The Sweeps	The Kaiser's Own
The Jaegers	

REGIMENTAL MARCHES

'Huntsman's Chorus'
'Lutzow's Wild Chase'

THIS famous Regiment was raised in America in 1755 and was recruited mainly from American colonists; the first Colonel was the Earl of Loudon, who happened to be the then Commander-in-Chief of the English forces in America.

The Regiment's first active service was against the French in Canada who, with their Red Indian allies, were actively engaged in hostilities against the British in America. The 60th Foot adopted light inconspicuous clothing and equipment (as compared with the standard red coats of Line Infantry); it adopted simple drill movements controlled by bugle calls – in fact, it took every possible step to ensure rapid movement combined with accuracy of shooting.

In 1759 the 60th Regiment of Foot, under Maj.-Gen. James Wolfe, played a leading role in the capture of Quebec, for which achievement it was awarded the motto *Celer et audax* ('Swift and bold').

The 60th fought with great distinction in the Peninsular War. Armed with the Baker rifle, the Regiment gave outstanding service in scouting, skirmishing, and protective roles – in all respects a model of speedy action and initiative.

The long record of service includes the campaign of the Crimea, and the Indian Mutiny, in which the 60th particularly distinguished itself at the Siege of Delhi (1857).

An interesting custom maintained by the Regiment is the sounding of 'ship's time' in barracks.

The 61st Regiment of Foot

THE GLOUCESTERSHIRE REGIMENT – 2ND BATTALION

PRECEDING TITLES

- 1756 2nd Battalion, The 3rd Regiment of Foot
- 1758 The 61st Regiment of Foot
- 1782 The 61st, South Gloucestershire Regiment
- 1881 2nd Battalion, The Gloucestershire Regiment

TODAY

See The 28th Regiment of Foot.

NICKNAMES

The Silver Tailed Dandies
The Flowers of Toulouse

REGIMENTAL MARCH

'The Highland Piper'

THE 61st Regiment of Foot was originally raised as the 2nd Battalion of the 3rd Regiment of Foot (The Buffs).

After some action in the West Indies the Regiment served in the Mediterranean, being at the memorable Siege of Minorca. The 61st also took part in the Egyptian Campaign of 1801 and, like the 28th, earned the battle honour 'Egypt' and the right to wear the Sphinx badge.

During the Peninsular War (1809) the 61st added more battle honours to its record, in particular 'Talavera'. At Toulouse (1814) it gained great glory and the nickname 'Flowers of Toulouse', said to have been given because of the spectacle presented by the 180 killed and wounded lying on the field of battle in their newly-issued scarlet uniforms. Salamanca (1812) was another battle where the 61st received unstinted praise for their gallantry.

The battle of Chillianwallah (1849) has been called the 'Waterloo of India', and in that battle the 61st Regiment fought with outstanding bravery against the Sikh Army, which outnumbered it by at least three to one. Then followed the Indian Mutiny, where the 61st Regiment distinguished itself at the Siege of Delhi.

The 62nd Regiment of Foot

THE WILTSHIRE REGIMENT
(DUKE OF EDINBURGH'S)

PRECEDING TITLES
1756   The 2nd Battalion, The 4th Regiment of Foot
1758   The 62nd Regiment of Foot
1782   The 62nd, or Wiltshire Regiment
1881   The Wiltshire Regiment (Duke of Edinburgh's)

On 9 June 1959 the Regiment linked with The Royal Berkshire Regiment, to form The Duke of Edinburgh's Royal Regiment (Berkshire and Wiltshire), which is a 'large' regiment of the Prince of Wales's Division.

NICKNAMES

The Springers
The Splashers
The Moonrakers

REGIMENTAL MARCHES

'The Wiltshire'	'The Farmer's Boy'
'The Poacher'	'The Vly be on the Turmits'
'May Blossoms' (slow)	'Rule, Britannia'

THERE had been three previous regiments called the 62nd, all disbanded or re-numbered, prior to the establishment of this predecessor of the Wiltshire Regiment.

In 1758 the Regiment served as marines during a sea-borne attack on French Canada. This service as marines was commemorated by the playing of 'Rule Britannia' after the regimental march. Later the Regiment acquired a ship's bell on which time was struck through the day, a most unusual custom in the British Army.

After service in Holland (1799) the 62nd was with Wellington's army in the Peninsula. It also gained great distinction at Sevastopol in the Crimean War.

The nickname 'Springers' arose from service as Light Infantry in the American campaign (1777). The 'Splashers' name, so it is said, stems from an incident in the defence of Carrickfergus Castle against the French in 1760. The story goes that the men ran out of bullets, and rammed their buttons down their muskets instead – at one time there was a 'splash' or dent in the uniform buttons of the 62nd Foot.

THE MANCHESTER REGIMENT

PRECEDING TITLES

    1756   2nd Battalion, Eighth, or The King's Regiment

    1758   The 63rd Regiment of Foot

    1783   The 63rd, West Suffolk, Regiment of Foot

    1881   The Manchester Regiment

TODAY

On 1 September 1958 the Regiment linked with The King's Regiment (Liverpool) to form The King's Regiment (Manchester and Liverpool). This Regiment became in 1969 The King's Regiment, part of the King's Division.

NICKNAMES

        The Blood Suckers

        The British Musketeers

REGIMENTAL MARCHES

        'The Young May Moon'

        'The Manchesters'

        'Farewell Manchester'

IT was in 1756 that a 2nd Battalion of the Eighth or King's Regiment was raised; in 1758 this Battalion was organised into a new regiment, the 63rd Regiment of Foot.

The history of this Regiment is closely associated with that of the King's Regiment (Manchester and Liverpool). They took part jointly in many engagements, including the War of American Independence and the Crimea. In particular, the 63rd Regiment gave outstanding service at Bunker's Hill (1775), Brooklyn (1776), Brandywine, and Fort Clinton (1777).

During the latter part of the eighteenth century the 63rd

Foot was frequently in direct conflict with the French. This fact may have led to the Regiment's adopting the fleur-de-lis device as a badge.

The fleur-de-lis, the French national emblem, was worn at Guadeloupe in 1759. However, it was not officially worn as a badge until 1930.

The 64th Regiment of Foot

THE NORTH STAFFORDSHIRE REGIMENT (THE PRINCE OF WALES'S)

PRECEDING TITLES
- 1756   The 2nd Battalion, the 11th Regiment of Foot
- 1758   The 64th (2nd Staffordshire) Regiment of Foot
- 1881   The North Staffordshire Regiment (The Prince of Wales's)

TODAY

On 31 January 1959 the Regiment linked with The South Staffordshire Regiment to form The Staffordshire Regiment (The Prince of Wales's), which is a 'large' regiment of the Prince of Wales's Division.

NICKNAME

The Black Knots

REGIMENTAL MARCHES

'Romaika'

'The Days We Went a-gypsying'

THE 64th Foot (originally the 2nd Battalion of the 11th

Foot) had as its first C.O. Col the Hon. John Barrington, who proved to be a very able and successful Colonel.

Two years after its formation (1758) the 64th Regiment went to the West Indies; there, together with the 38th Regiment (with whom they were ultimately linked in 1959) they served in many engagements in Guadeloupe and Martinique.

The 64th saw action in the War of American Independence (1780), but they arrived in Belgium too late to serve at Waterloo. But the 64th was one of the few British regiments available in India at the outbreak of the Mutiny (1857). It saw action at Cawnpore, and with Gen. Havelock, taking part in the Relief of Lucknow. The Regiment's first Victoria Cross was won by Drummer Thomas Flynn who displayed outstanding courage during an attack on the enemy guns at Cawnpore.

The 64th Foot shared one of its badges with the 38th Foot – the Staffordshire knot device. It also bears the Prince of Wales's plumes.

The Regiment used to have black facings, which was probably the reason for the nickname

The 65th Regiment of Foot

THE YORK AND LANCASTER REGIMENT

PRECEDING TITLES

    1756   The 2nd Battalion, The 12th Regiment of Foot
    1758   The 65th Regiment of Foot
    1782   The 65th, or the 2nd Yorkshire North Riding Regiment
    1881   The York and Lancaster Regiment

In 1957 the Regiment became the fourth regiment in seniority in the Yorkshire Brigade, the King's Division, but was disbanded on 14 December 1968.

NICKNAMES

The Royal Tigers

The Twin Roses

The Cat and Cabbage

The Ickety Pips

The Young and Lovelies

REGIMENTAL MARCH

'The York and Lancaster'

IN 1756, on the outbreak of the Seven Years' War with France, the 12th Foot raised a 2nd Battalion in Suffolk. This battalion became a separate regiment numbered the 65th in 1758. The first Commanding Officer was Sir Robert Armiger.

The 65th saw service in the West Indies, and followed this with action in the War of American Independence, including the Battle of Bunker's Hill (1775).

Following this, the 65th Foot served with great distinction in India during the early part of the nineteenth century. It took part in the Mahratta Wars of 1805 and 1817 and various expeditions against the Arab pirates of the Persian Gulf.

On the return of the Regiment to England (1822) it was granted the badge of the Royal Tiger in recognition of its service (*London Gazette*, 12 April 1823). The words 'India' and 'Arabia' were included in the award – in fact the 65th is the only British regiment to bear 'Arabia' as a battle honour.

The 65th Foot later served in New Zealand (1846–65), taking part in the Maori Wars. Two Victoria Crosses were awarded during the campaigns.

One of the nicknames, 'Ickety Pips', is said to have arisen from the Maori pronunciation of '65th'.

THE ROYAL BERKSHIRE REGIMENT (PRINCESS CHARLOTTE OF WALES'S) – 2ND BATTALION

PRECEDING TITLES

    1756   The 2nd Battalion, The 19th Regiment of Foot

    1758   The 66th Regiment of Foot

    1782   The 66th, or Berkshire Regiment

    1881   2nd Battalion, Princess Charlotte of Wales's Berkshire Regiment

TODAY

    See The 49th Regiment of Foot.

NICKNAME

       The Brave Boys of Berks

REGIMENTAL MARCH

       'The Farmer's Boy'

THE 19th Regiment of Foot (later to become The Green Howards) raised a 2nd Battalion at the time of the outbreak of the Seven Years' War (1756); this battalion, two years later, became a regiment in its own right and was re-numbered the 66th Regiment of Foot.

It saw active service in the Peninsular War under Wellington, gaining, among others, the battle honours 'Douro', 'Talavera', 'Albuera', and 'Vittoria'. In 1816 it served at St Helena on garrison duty guarding Napoleon after his defeat at Waterloo.

The 66th Regiment of Foot suffered severe casualties at the Battle of Maiwand in Afghanistan (1880). A total of six companies of the Regiment were almost totally annihilated; one survivor of that battle, however, is on display in the regimental museum. He is Bobbie, the pet dog of one of the sergeants – in 1881 Queen Victoria granted Bobbie an audience and presented him with the Afghan Medal. But the next year, unfortunately, he was run over by a cab. He was then stuffed, and now sits in the museum, complete with his medal.

The 67th Regiment of Foot

THE ROYAL HAMPSHIRE REGIMENT – 2ND BATTALION

PRECEDING TITLES

1756　2nd Battalion, The 20th Regiment of Foot
1758　The 67th Regiment of Foot
1782　The 67th (South Hampshire) Regiment of Foot
1881　2nd Battalion, The Hampshire Regiment
1946　2nd Battalion, The Royal Hampshire Regiment

TODAY
　　See the 37th Regiment of Foot.

NICKNAME
　　　　The Hampshire Tigers

REGIMENTAL MARCH
　　　　'We'll Gang Nae Mair to yon Toun'

THE Regiment destined to be the 'father' of the 67th Regiment of Foot was itself raised in 1688; in 1756 fifteen of the then line regiments were authorised to raise 2nd battalions, and of these, it was the 2nd Battalion of the 20th Foot that became the 67th Regiment in the order of seniority.

James Wolfe (of Quebec fame) was the first Colonel. The Regiment saw service in Minorca (1763) and the

West Indies, and spent some twenty-one years in India (1805–26). As previously mentioned, George IV added the Bengal Tiger to the Regiment's badge as a recognition of its Indian service.

The next thirty years were uneventfully spent in England, Ireland, Gibraltar, the West Indies, and Canada. Then followed service in the Far East; the Regiment gained its first four Victoria Crosses at the storming of the Taku Forts (1860).

The 68th Regiment of Foot

THE DURHAM LIGHT INFANTRY

PRECEDING TITLES
- 1756   The 2nd Battalion, The 23rd Regiment of Foot
- 1758   The 68th Regiment of Foot
- 1783   The 68th, or Durham Regiment
- 1808   The 68th, or Durham Regiment, Light Infantry
- 1881   The Durham Light Infantry

TODAY

In 1968 the Regiment became part of the 'large' Light Infantry Regiment, Light Division. The Durham Light Infantry was disbanded in December of the same year.

NICKNAME

The Faithful Durhams

REGIMENTAL MARCHES

'The Light Barque'
'The Old 68th'
'The Keel Row'

RAISED by Col John Lambton (grandfather of the first Earl of Durham), this Regiment was stationed in the West Indies in 1772 and suffered severe losses from yellow fever. Probably it was their faithful service in this tropical climate that gave rise to the nickname.

In 1808 the Regiment was the third to be converted to Light Infantry, and it joined Wellington's army in Portugal in 1811. It fought at Salamanca, Vittoria, Nivelle, and Orthez in the Peninsular War, gaining well-deserved battle honours.

The Crimean War was the next scene of action – 'Alma', 'Inkerman', and 'Sevastopol' were added to the battle honours. At Inkerman Pte John Byrne of the 68th won the first Victoria Cross to be awarded during the Crimean campaign. It is also recorded that in this battle the 68th was the only English regiment to fight in red coats. In 1885 the 68th, now the Durham Light Infantry, took part in the Sudan campaign at the Battle of Ginnis, memorable as being the last time British infantry fought in red.

The 69th Regiment of Foot

THE WELCH REGIMENT – 2ND BATTALION

PRECEDING TITLES

See The 41st Regiment of Foot.

The Old Agamemnons
The Ups and Downs
Wardour's Horse

'Ap Shenkin'

IN 1756 fifteen infantry regiments were authorised to raise 2nd battalions. Of these, the 24th Foot raised a 2nd Battalion which became a separate regiment in 1758, and was numbered the 69th Regiment of Foot. Most of the men were recruited from Nottinghamshire, Derbyshire, and Lancashire.

The Regiment saw service in the West Indies and was at the capture of St Lucia in 1778. Then followed a period of service as a marine corps in 1782.

Indeed the 69th Regiment of Foot gave outstanding service as marines in a number of naval actions during the years 1793–7. These included the Siege of Genoa, the capture of Porto Ferrajo, Leghorn, and Laona Bay.

Men of the 69th Foot served in H.M.S. *Agamemnon* under Nelson (1793–6). It was Nelson himself who gave them the nickname 'Old Agamemnons'. At the Battle of St Vincent (1797) Nelson had a detachment of men of the 69th Regiment on board his ship H.M.S. *Captain*, and one of these men – Pte Matthew Stevens – was among the first to board the Spanish ship *San Nicholas*.

It is said that the nickname 'the Ups and Downs' comes from the fact that '69' can be read just as well upside down.

THE EAST SURREY REGIMENT – 2ND BATTALION

PRECEDING TITLES

1756   The 2nd Battalion, The 31st Regiment of Foot
1758   The 70th Regiment of Foot
1782   The 70th, Surrey Regiment
1812   The 70th, Glasgow Lowland Regiment
1825   The 70th (Surrey) Regiment
1881   The 2nd Battalion, The East Surrey Regiment

TODAY
See The 31st Regiment of Foot.

NICKNAME
The Glasgow Greys

REGIMENTAL MARCH
'Lass o' Gowrie'

THIS Regiment was originally raised in 1756 as the 2nd Battalion of the 31st Foot, but was later designated the 70th Regiment of Foot. It served with distinction in the West Indies (1794), and under Sir Charles Grey was at the capture of Guadaloupe and Martinique.

The 70th Foot also fought in the Maori Wars of 1863–6, having been engaged in operations in New Zealand since June 1861.

The nickname 'Glasgow Greys' is said to originate from the fact that the Regiment was raised (as the 2nd Battalion of the 31st Foot) in Glasgow. When it became a separate Regiment in 1758 it was still stationed in Scotland, and had adopted grey facings to its uniform. These grey facings were changed to black in 1768.

THE HIGHLAND LIGHT INFANTRY (CITY OF GLASGOW REGIMENT)

PRECEDING TITLES

1777　The 73rd Highland Regiment of Foot (Lord MacLeod's Highlanders)

1786　The 71st Highland Regiment of Foot

1808　The 71st, Glasgow Highland Regiment

1809　The 71st, Glasgow Highland Light Infantry

1810　The 71st, Highland Light Infantry

1881　The Highland Light Infantry (City of Glasgow Regiment)

TODAY

On 20 January 1959 the Regiment amalgamated with The Royal Scots Fusiliers to form The Royal Highland Fusiliers (Princess Margaret's Own Glasgow and Ayrshire Regiment), part of the Scottish Division.

NICKNAMES

The Pig and Whistle Light Infantry
The Glesca Kilties

REGIMENTAL MARCHES

'Whistle o'er the Lave o't'
'Blue Bonnets over the Border'

IN 1777 King George II gave a commission to John MacKenzie, Lord MacLeod, to raise a regiment of foot. The Regiment, the 73rd Highlanders, was the first 'clan' regiment to be raised, and proudly wore the MacKenzie tartan.

The Regiment was re-numbered the 71st Highlanders in 1786: as a matter of interest there had been three previous 71st Regiments, known as 'Fraser's Highlanders', but they had no connection with MacLeod's Highlanders and were all disbanded about 1775–6.

As the 73rd, the Regiment served in India for the Honourable East India Company during the Mysore campaigns (1779); as the 71st it took part in the invasion of Ceylon (1795–6).

South Africa (1805) was followed by South America in 1806. Then followed the Peninsular campaign, where the 71st distinguished itself at Rolica, Vimeiro (1808), and Corunna (1809).

As Light Infantry the Regiment served in the second Peninsular campaign. It was also at Waterloo, the Crimea, and the Indian Mutiny.

The 72nd Regiment of Foot

THE SEAFORTH HIGHLANDERS (ROSS-SHIRE BUFFS, THE DUKE OF ALBANY'S)

PRECEDING TITLES

- 1778 The 78th Highland Regiment (Lord Seaforth's Highlanders)
- 1786 The 72nd Highland Regiment of Foot
- 1823 The 72nd, The Duke of Albany's Own Highlanders
- 1881 The Seaforth Highlanders (Ross-shire Buffs, The Duke of Albany's)

TODAY

On 7 February 1961 the Regiment amalgamated with The Queen's Own Cameron Highlanders to form The Queen's Own Highlanders (Seaforth and Cameron), a 'large' regiment of the Scottish Division.

The Macraes

'Highland Laddie'

In May 1778, at the time of the War of American Independence, the Earl of Seaforth raised a regiment of foot at Elgin. It was numbered the 78th, and placed on the Establishment as Lord Seaforth's Highlanders; in 1786 the Regiment was re-numbered '72'.

After action in the Channel Islands (1778–9) the Regiment went to India (1782) and took part in the siege of the French fortress at Cuddalore. Some of the men of the 72nd served as marines in a naval action against the French fleet.

Then followed campaigns against Tippoo Sahib (1789), Pondicherry (1793), and Ceylon (1795–7). After home service, the 72nd fought against the Dutch in South Africa (1806), and then served in the West Indies (1810–14).

In 1823 King George IV granted the Regiment the title 'The Duke of Albany's Own Highlanders'. The King's brother, Frederick, Duke of York and Albany, was Commander-in-Chief of the Army at that time.

The 72nd Regiment of Foot fought in the Crimea (1854), the Indian Mutiny (1857), and the Afghan War (1878), winning many well-deserved battle honours.

The Regiment's badge, together with the motto *Cuidich 'n Righ* ('Help the King'), is the crest of the Seaforth family: the crest and motto were awarded to Colin Fitzgerald, an ancestor of the Earl of Seaforth, in the year 1255 for saving the life of King Alexander III of Scotland when he was in danger of being savaged by an infuriated stag in the Mar Forest.

The Regiment's nickname arose from the extraordinary number of Macraes who enlisted in it in its early years.

THE BLACK WATCH
(ROYAL HIGHLAND REGIMENT) –
2ND BATTALION

PRECEDING TITLES

1758 and 1779	2nd Battalion, 42nd (Royal Highland) Regiment of Foot
1786	The 73rd Highland Regiment of Foot
1809	The 73rd Regiment of Foot
1862	The 73rd (Perthshire) Regiment
1881	2nd Battalion, The Black Watch (Royal Highlanders)
1934	2nd Battalion, The Black Watch (Royal Highland Regiment)

TODAY

See The 42nd Regiment of Foot.

NICKNAME

(None recorded)

REGIMENTAL MARCH

'Highland Laddie'

THE 73rd Foot was originally raised in Perth (1758) as the 2nd Battalion of the 42nd Regiment of Foot; after service in the West Indies and Canada, the Battalion was disbanded in 1762. It was raised again in 1779, with the same designation.

The Battalion served in India under Col Norman Macleod, campaigning against Haidar Ali and his son Tippoo Sahib: one of its outstanding engagements was the siege and capture of Mangalore (May 1783).

In 1786 the 2nd Battalion, 42nd Foot, was designated the

73rd Highlanders; it continued under this title until 1881 when, as a result of the Cardwell Reforms, it was once again linked with the 42nd Foot, now The Black Watch.

The 73rd Regiment of Foot has a record of service covering many engagements in India and Ceylon. Serving with the Regiment at that time was a young Ensign, Arthur Wellesley, who later reached the rank of Colonel, and commanded the Regiment in 1779. It was, of course, to know him again later as the Duke of Wellington.

The heroic display of devotion to duty given by some young recruits of the 73rd Regiment at the wreck of the *Birkenhead* in 1852 is remembered with honour: fifty-six men sacrificed their lives to ensure that not one woman or child was drowned. The German Kaiser himself ordered a report of the troops' gallant behaviour to be read to all regiments of the German Army as a supreme example of discipline and courage.

The 74th Regiment of Foot

THE HIGHLAND LIGHT INFANTRY (CITY OF GLASGOW REGIMENT) – 2ND BATTALION

PRECEDING TITLES

1787   The 74th (Highland) Regiment of Foot
1816   The 74th Regiment of Foot
1845   The 74th (Highlanders) Regiment
1881   2nd Battalion, The Highland Light Infantry
           (City of Glasgow Regiment)

See The 71st Regiment of Foot.

The 'Assaye' Regiment
The Assayes

REGIMENTAL MARCH
'Blue Bonnets over the Border'

THE 74th Regiment of Foot was raised in Argyll by Sir Archibald Campbell of Inverniel in 1787. There had been three previous 74th Regiments (Argyll Highlanders) between 1777 and 1783, but all were later disbanded, and none had any connection with Campbell's Highlanders.

The Regiment's first action was the second Mysore campaign (1789), where it took part in the Battle of Bangalore (1791) and Seringapatam (1792).

In the Mahratta War (1802-5) the 74th, under Sir Arthur Wellesley, fought with great distinction, particularly at Assaye (1803); for this action the Regiment was granted the 'Assaye' Colour by The Honourable East India Company. This was a special honorary Colour, for many years trooped on Assaye Day, and eventually laid up in Glasgow Cathedral in 1882.

The 74th took part in the Peninsular campaign, the Kaffir Wars, and the Indian Mutiny; in 1852 the 74th was the Regiment which had the largest draft of troops on board the ill-fated transport *Birkenhead*. Under the command of Lt-Col Seaton the men kept their ranks until the ship sank beneath them, their bravery and self-control helping to ensure the safety of all the women and children on board.

The 75th Regiment of Foot

THE GORDON HIGHLANDERS

PRECEDING TITLES

1787   The 75th (Highland) Regiment of Foot
1804   The 75th Regiment of Foot
1862   The 75th, The Stirlingshire Regiment
1881   The Gordon Highlanders

TODAY

The Regiment is now part of the Scottish Division.

NICKNAME

The Gay Gordons

REGIMENTAL MARCHES

'Cock of the North'
'Highland Laddie'

THE 75th Regiment of Foot (originally known as Abercromby's Highlanders) was raised in 1787 by Sir Robert Abercromby in Stirling. There had been three previous 75th Regiments, all of very short duration, and all disbanded before the raising of Abercromby's Regiment.

Very shortly after being raised the Regiment was on active service in India; it fought with outstanding gallantry at Seringapatam and Mysore, gaining well-deserved battle honours (1799). King George III granted the Regiment the right to bear on its Colours the Royal Tiger and the word 'India'.

The Regiment served in the Mediterranean, and was active in the Kaffir Wars (1832), winning another battle honour. The Indian Mutiny (1857–8) was its next campaign – this was when Ensign Wadeson won the V.C. at Delhi.

In the years following the link with the 92nd Foot, the Gordon Highlanders gained many more battle honours: in the Egyptian Wars (1882), the Sudan (1883–4), and in India on the North-West Frontier.

THE DUKE OF WELLINGTON'S REGIMENT (WEST RIDING) – 2ND BATTALION

PRECEDING TITLES
1787   The 76th Regiment of Foot
1807   The 76th (Hindoostan) Regiment of Foot
1812   The 76th Regiment of Foot
1881   2nd Battalion, The Duke of Wellington's Regiment (West Riding)

TODAY
See The 33rd Regiment of Foot.

NICKNAMES
> The Immortals   The Hindoostan Regiment
> The Pigs   The Seven and Sixpennies

REGIMENTAL MARCH
> 'The Wellesley'

BEFORE the present Regiment there had been a previous 76th Regiment of Foot, raised in 1777, and known as 'Macdonald's Highlanders'. It was disbanded in 1784.

The present Regiment, raised in 1787 by the East India Company at Chatham, had as its first Colonel Lord Harris, the victor of Seringapatam: it also had, as an attached subaltern, one Arthur Wesley – the future Duke of Wellington. (The great man reverted to the name Wellesley only after his arrival in India in 1789.) The 76th Foot served twenty years in India (1787–1807) and was granted the elephant in its badge in recognition of this service. The nickname 'Pigs' is said to have arisen from this emblem. The Regiment had a special pair of Colours presented by The Honourable East India Company –

again in recognition of its distinguished service in India.

The 76th saw considerable service in the Pyrenees under the Duke of Wellington, including engagements at Bidassoa, the Nive, Adour, and Bayonne.

The nickname 'Immortals' arises – so tradition has it – from the fact that during Lake's campaign in India most of the men in the Regiment were wounded, but hardly any fatally.

The 77th Regiment of Foot

THE MIDDLESEX REGIMENT (DUKE OF CAMBRIDGE'S OWN) – 2ND BATTALION

PRECEDING TITLES

1787   The 77th (East Middlesex) Regiment of Foot

1876   The 77th (East Middlesex) Duke of Cambridge's Own Regiment

1881   2nd Battalion, The Middlesex Regiment (Duke of Cambridge's Own)

TODAY

See The 57th Regiment of Foot.

NICKNAME

The Pot Hooks

REGIMENTAL MARCH

'Paddy's Resource'

THERE had been two earlier regiments carrying the number 77; they were the Montgomery and the Atholl Highlanders, and flourished between 1778 and 1783.

The 77th Regiment of Foot discussed here was raised in 1787, and was originally intended for service in Canada. The War of American Independence had finished in 1783 and despite the strained relations still existing between England and America, the 77th did not sail for the North American continent.

The Regiment gave valiant service at Martinique and Havannah in the West Indies. In the Peninsular War, the 77th was one of the regiments which stormed Cuidad Rodrigo; it displayed bravery and ferocity in attack at least equal to that of the 57th Regiment – with which it was linked in 1881.

In all, the 77th spent over twenty years in India: it served under Lord Cornwallis in the campaign against Tippoo Sahib (1790–1); it served in Ceylon (1795) and Goa (1799); and its activities included some distinguished action at the storming and capture of Seringapatam.

The 78th Regiment of Foot

THE SEAFORTH HIGHLANDERS (ROSS-SHIRE BUFFS, THE DUKE OF ALBANY'S) – 2ND BATTALION

PRECEDING TITLES

   1793   The 78th Highland Regiment of Foot
   1794   The 78th, Ross-shire Buffs
   1881   2nd Battalion, The Seaforth Highlanders (Ross-shire Buffs, The Duke of Albany's)

TODAY

   See The 72nd Regiment of Foot.

NICKNAME

      The King's Men

'Highland Laddie'

IN 1793 the Earl of Seaforth's cousin, Francis Humberstone Mackenzie, raised a regiment of foot at Fort George. The Regiment was given rank as the 78th Foot, and in 1794 it was in action in the Netherlands.

After service at the Cape of Good Hope (1795), the Regiment went to India (1797), where in 1803, under Maj.-Gen. the Hon. Arthur Wellesley, it fought against the Mahrattas; for this service it was rewarded with the distinction 'Assaye' and an honorary third Colour presented by The Honourable East India Company.

The 78th fought the French at Maida (1806) and again in Java (1811); next came home service, followed by Ceylon, India, and Aden. It distinguished itself highly at Waterloo, and served under Gen. Havelock in the Indian Mutiny, being present at the storming of Cawnpore and taking part in the Relief of Lucknow. It is on record that during the Mutiny eight men of the 78th won the Victoria Cross.

The nickname carried by this famous Regiment is said to be related to the motto in the crest of the Seaforth family, *Cuidich 'n Righ* ('Help the King').

The 79th Regiment of Foot

THE QUEEN'S OWN CAMERON HIGHLANDERS

PRECEDING TITLES

1793   The 79th, Cameronian Volunteers
1794   The 79th Regiment, Cameron Highlanders
1805   The 79th Regiment of Foot
1807   The 79th, Cameron Highlanders

1873   The 79th, The Queen's Own Cameron High-
       landers
1881   The Queen's Own Cameron Highlanders

TODAY

On 7 February 1961 the Regiment linked with The
Seaforth Highlanders to form The Queen's Own
Highlanders (Seaforth and Cameron), a 'large' regi-
ment of the Scottish Division.

NICKNAME
       (None recorded)

REGIMENTAL MARCHES
       'March of the Cameron Men'
       'Pibroch o' Doniul Dhu'
       'Highland Laddie'

MAJOR ALAN CAMERON OF ERRACHT (later Lt-Gen. Sir
Alan Cameron, K.C.B.) raised the 79th Regiment of Foot
on 17 August 1793. There had been two previous 79th
Regiments, both of them disbanded after a short existence.

In 1794 the Regiment served with the Duke of York's
army in Holland and won its first battle honour at Egmont-
op-Zee (1799). Under Sir Ralph Abercromby it served in
the Egyptian campaign, and for this was rewarded with
the right to wear the Sphinx superscribed 'Egypt'.

The Regiment greatly distinguished itself in the Peninsular War, routing the French Imperial Guard at Fuentes
de Onoro; serving throughout this campaign, the 79th
gained many more battle honours; its Light Company
fought at Corunna.

The 79th Regiment was the first to leave Brussels on the
morning of 16 June 1815, and was publicly praised by
Wellington for its behaviour at Quatre Bras and Waterloo.
Then followed gallant service in the Crimea, the Indian
Mutiny, Egypt (1882), and the Sudan (1893).

The Camerons were the only Highland regiment unaffected by the Cardwell Reforms as regards dress; they were permitted to retain their own Erracht tartan.

On 17 April 1873 Queen Victoria commanded that the Regiment be titled 'The 79th, The Queen's Own Cameron Highlanders', and that the facing be changed from green to blue. At the same time the Regiment was granted the special badge of the Thistle with Imperial Crown, 'as being the Badge of Scotland sanctioned by Queen Anne in 1707 on the confirmation of the Act of Union between the two Kingdoms'.

The 8oth Regiment of Foot

THE SOUTH STAFFORDSHIRE REGIMENT – 2ND BATTALION

PRECEDING TITLES

1793　The 8oth, or Staffordshire Volunteers' Regiment
1881　2nd Battalion, The South Staffordshire Regiment

TODAY

See The 38th Regiment of Foot.

NICKNAMES

The Staffordshire Knots
Gage's Light Infantry

REGIMENTAL MARCHES

'Come Lasses and Lads'
'The 8oth' (slow)

THERE had been two previous 8oth Regiments, both disbanded prior to the raising of the Staffordshire Volunteers by Lord Henry William Paget (later first Marquis of Anglesey) in 1793. This distinguished soldier was later Wellington's second-in-command at Waterloo, in which battle he lost a leg.

The Regiment fought in the dreadful Flanders campaign of 1794–5, following this by service in the war in Egypt (1801). It was here that it received the battle honour of the Sphinx, superscribed 'Egypt'. In 1852 the 80th Foot was again on active service in the Second Burma War, taking part in the storming of Rangoon, Pegu, and Prome. Among the officers of the Regiment who were severely wounded was Ensign Wolseley, later to become the famous General of the Victorian era.

The 80th saw service in India during the Mutiny (1858). In the Zulu War (1878) a mounted infantry detachment of the 80th was at the Battle of Isandhlwana (1879): one of the survivors of this tragic engagement was Pte W. Wassal, whose heroism earned the award of the Victoria Cross – the first V.C. to be won by the South Staffordshire Regiment.

In transit the 80th Foot seemed to be singularly unlucky. Three times they were shipwrecked in troop-ships, once losing all their records and mess silver.

The 81st Regiment of Foot

THE LOYAL REGIMENT
(NORTH LANCASHIRE) – 2ND
BATTALION

PRECEDING TITLES

1793 The 81st, Loyal Lincoln Volunteers Regiment

1794 The 81st Regiment of Foot

1832 The 81st Regiment of Foot (Loyal Lincoln Volunteers)

1881   2nd Battalion, The Loyal North Lancashire Regiment

1921   2nd Battalion, The Loyal Regiment (North Lancashire)

TODAY

See The 47th Regiment of Foot.

NICKNAME

Loyal Lincoln Volunteers

REGIMENTAL MARCHES

'The Red, Red Rose'
'The Lincolnshire Poacher'

COL ALBERMARLE BERTIE of the 1st Foot Guards (he was later the sixth Earl of Lindsay) raised this Regiment at Lincoln on 23 September 1793. (There had been a previous 81st Regiment, the Aberdeenshire Highland Regiment, raised in 1777 and disbanded in 1783.)

So rapid and willing was the response to the call for recruits when the Regiment was raised that this may be the origin of the nickname 'Loyal Lincoln Volunteers'; alternatively, the term 'Loyal' may have come from Col Bertie's motto, *Loyauté m'oblige*. In any case, it was the 81st Regiment that contributed the 'Loyal' to the title of the combined 47th/81st Regiment in 1881. The 'Lincolnshire Poacher' march is obviously connected with the fact that the Regiment was raised in Lincoln.

Its first active service was in the West Indies (1793–7), followed by five years at the Cape of Good Hope. The Regiment won its first battle honour at Maida (1806), and after service in eastern Spain (1812), Canada (1814), and other overseas postings, the 81st was in India at the time of the Indian Mutiny (1852).

The Regiment also fought in the second Afghan War (1874). It linked with the 47th Foot to form the Loyal North Lancashire Regiment in 1881.

THE SOUTH LANCASHIRE REGIMENT (THE PRINCE OF WALES'S VOLUNTEERS) – 2ND BATTALION

PRECEDING TITLES

1793   The 82nd (The Prince of Wales's Volunteers)
Regiment of Foot

1881   2nd Battalion, The South Lancashire Regiment
(The Prince of Wales's Volunteers)

TODAY
See The 40th Regiment of Foot.

NICKNAME
The Powos

REGIMENTAL MARCH
'God Bless the Prince of Wales'

THERE had been two 82nd Regiments earlier in the century, but they were disbanded in, respectively, 1763 and 1784.

The present 82nd Regiment was raised in 1793 by Maj.-Gen. Leigh, who himself belonged to the 3rd Foot Guards. Gen. Leigh was a member of the entourage of the Prince of Wales – hence the Regiment was given the title 'The Prince of Wales's Volunteers' and the appropriate coronet and plume in the badge.

The Regiment fought with great distinction at Rolica, Vimeiro, and Corunna. Its outstanding bravery in action at the Pass of Maya (1813) earned a special commendation from Wellington.

Then followed a period of service in Mauritius (1819), and from 1837 to 1839 the Regiment was stationed at Gibraltar. Jamaica was the next posting, and here the

117

Regiment suffered severely from the ravages of yellow fever.

The Regiment then served in Canada (1843–7). At the outbreak of the Indian Mutiny it was sent to India, and there played a prominent part in the Relief of Lucknow.

The 83rd Regiment of Foot

THE ROYAL ULSTER RIFLES

PRECEDING TITLES

- 1793   The 83rd Regiment of Foot
- 1859   The 83rd (County of Dublin) Regiment of Foot
- 1881   The Royal Irish Rifles
- 1921   The Royal Ulster Rifles

TODAY

On 1 July 1968 The Royal Ulster Rifles merged with The Royal Irish Fusiliers (Princess Victoria's) and The Royal Inniskilling Fusiliers to form The Royal Irish Rangers, a 'large' regiment of the King's Division.

NICKNAME

Fitch's Grenadiers

REGIMENTAL MARCHES

'Garryowen'
' "Off," said the Stranger'

ON 28 September 1793 Lt-Col William Fitch (late of the 55th Regiment of Foot) raised the 83rd Regiment in Dublin.

After three years' campaigning in the West Indies (1795–8), during which the Regiment suffered the tragic loss of its Commanding Officer, Col Fitch, the 83rd played a major role in the almost continuous warfare with France which ended with the defeat of Napoleon at Waterloo (1815). In particular it gained many battle honours in the

Peninsular War, notably at Talavera (1809), Busaco (1810), Badajos (1812), and Salamanca.

The 83rd Regiment was in Bombay on the outbreak of the Indian Mutiny (1857–9), and in the ensuing campaign gave outstanding service in many actions against the rebels.

In 1859, in formal recognition of the connection with the Regiment's place of raising, Queen Victoria granted it the title 'County of Dublin' Regiment.

The nickname 'Fitch's Grenadiers' merits an explanation: grenadiers were, by tradition, always chosen from the tallest troops. Col Fitch's men were mostly of diminutive stature – hence the ironic sobriquet.

The 84th Regiment of Foot

THE YORK AND LANCASTER REGIMENT – 2ND BATTALION

PRECEDING TITLES

    1793   The 84th Regiment of Foot

    1809   The 84th Foot, or York and Lancaster Regiment

    1881   2nd Battalion, The York and Lancaster Regiment

TODAY

    See The 65th Regiment of Foot.

NICKNAMES

        The Young and Lovelies

        The Rabbit and Geranium

        The Cork and Doncaster

REGIMENTAL MARCH

        'The Jockey of York'

THERE were two previous regiments of foot carrying the number '84'. One was raised in 1759 by Sir Eyre Coote, and this, after service in India, was disbanded in 1763. The second was raised in Canada on the outbreak of the War of American Independence (1775), and was recruited mainly from loyal Scottish settlers. It was named the 84th (Royal Highland Emigrant) Regiment, and was disbanded at the end of hostilities.

The present 84th Foot was raised in 1793 on the outbreak of war with revolutionary France. Following active service in the Netherlands, the Regiment was in India from 1798 to 1819, taking part in the Mahratta and Pindari Wars.

In 1809 the 84th Foot was granted the second title 'York and Lancaster Regiment', and in 1820 it was granted the badge of the Union Rose.

During the Indian Mutiny (1857) the Regiment served with outstanding distinction at Cawnpore, and at both the defence and the Relief of Lucknow, suffering severe losses. Six members of the 84th were awarded the Victoria Cross, and the Regiment received the battle honour 'Lucknow'.

The 85th Regiment of Foot

THE KING'S SHROPSHIRE LIGHT INFANTRY – 2ND BATTALION

PRECEDING TITLES

1794 The 85th (Bucks Volunteers) Regiment of Foot

1808 The 85th (Bucks Volunteers) Light Infantry

1815 The 85th (Bucks Volunteers) Duke of York's Own Light Infantry

1821 The 85th (Bucks Volunteers) King's Light Infantry

1881 2nd Battalion, The King's Shropshire Light Infantry

See The 53rd Regiment of Foot.

The Young Bucks
The Elegant Extracts

'Daughter of the Regiment'

THE 85th Regiment of Foot was raised by Lt-Col Nugent (later Field-Marshal Sir George Nugent) in Aylesbury, Buckinghamshire, in 1793–4. The Marquis of Buckingham was Col Nugent's cousin, and it was the great interest of the Marquis which led to that area being chosen as the site of the raising.

There had been two previous 85th Regiments, both disbanded after comparatively short existences – the original 85th, raised in 1759 as the Regiment of Royal Volontiers, had the distinction of being the first Light Infantry regiment to be formed in the British Army.

After service in Holland and the West Indies, the Bucks Volunteers were formed into Light Infantry (1808), and then served in the Peninsular War, giving outstanding performances at Fuentes de Onoro and Badajoz. The 85th were next engaged in action in America (1814–15), and were stationed in Ireland during the great potato famine of 1846.

The nickname 'Elegant Extracts' has its origin in internal dissensions on personal matters among the officers of the 85th; in 1813 a series of courts martial led to the removal of all officers (except the C.O.) to other regiments. All the new officers were drawn from other regiments and were known, until fairly recent times, as the 'Elegant Extracts'.

THE ROYAL ULSTER RIFLES
– 2ND BATTALION

PRECEDING TITLES

1793	Cuyler's Shropshire Volunteers
1794	The 86th, Shropshire Volunteers
1806	The 86th, Leinster Regiment of Foot
1812	The 86th (Royal County Down) Regiment of Foot
1881	2nd Battalion, The Royal Irish Rifles
1921	2nd Battalion, The Royal Ulster Rifles

TODAY

See The 83rd Regiment of Foot.

NICKNAME

The Irish Giants

REGIMENTAL MARCH

'St Patrick's Day'

MAJ.-GEN. SIR CORNELIUS CUYLER raised the 86th Regiment of Foot in Shropshire on 2 November 1793. Shortly after its formation the Regiment moved to Ireland, where the number '86' was officially allotted, replacing the clumsy original title 'Cuyler's Shropshire Volunteers'.

The Regiment's first active service was as marines in ships of the Line against the French Navy (1795). After service at the Cape of Good Hope (1796), the Regiment served in India (1799), and in Egypt (1801), where it played a major part in the defeat of the French Army; for this the 86th received, by royal authority, the Sphinx emblem superscribed 'Egypt'.

In 1802 the 86th Regiment of Foot, together with forces of The Honourable East India Company, fought valiantly in the Mahratta Wars. In 1806 it was officially named the 'Leinster Regiment' (no one really knows why), and in 1812, in recognition of its capture of the French island of Bourbon, the Regiment was retitled the 'Royal County Down' Regiment of Foot – the battle honour 'Bourbon' had been awarded in 1810.

During the Indian Mutiny, at the storming of the Fort of Jhansi (April 1858), men of the 86th Regiment won no less than four Victoria Crosses.

The Regiment's nickname 'Irish Giants' is said to have been given to it because of the fine physique of the men.

The 87th Regiment of Foot

THE ROYAL IRISH FUSILIERS (PRINCESS VICTORIA'S)

PRECEDING TITLES

1793 The 87th (The Prince of Wales's) Irish Regiment of Foot

1811 The 87th (The Prince of Wales's Own) Irish Regiment of Foot

1827 The 87th (The Prince of Wales's Own) Irish (May) Fusiliers

1827 The 87th, The Royal Irish Fusiliers (November)

1881 Princess Victoria's (The Royal Irish Fusiliers)

1920 The Royal Irish Fusiliers (Princess Victoria's)

TODAY

On 1 July 1968 the Regiment linked with The Royal Ulster Rifles and The Royal Inniskilling Fusiliers to form The Royal Irish Rangers, which is a 'large' regiment of the King's Division.

The Eagle Takers   The 'Aiglers'
The Faugh-a-   The Fogs (or Faughs)
Ballagh Boys

REGIMENTAL MARCHES
'St Patrick's Day'
'Nora Creina'
'The British Grenadiers'

THE 87th Regiment of Foot was raised as the Prince of Wales's Irish Regiment towards the end of 1793 by Lt-Col John Doyle (later Gen. Sir John Doyle, Bart, G.C.B.). The number '87' had, however, been used earlier by two short-lived Scottish Regiments, Keith's and Campbell's Highlanders, between 1759 and 1763.

After action in Flanders (1794), the 87th Regiment of Foot served in the West Indies (1796), followed by South America (1807), and India – the little-known Gurkha War of 1815–16.

The Peninsular War saw the 87th winning battle honours and glory at Talavera, Barrosa, and Vittoria; it was at Barrosa (1811) that the 2nd Battalion succeeded in capturing the Eagle Standard of the French 8th Regiment of Grenadiers. At Vittoria it captured the baton of the French Marshal Jourdan.

The nicknames 'the Faughs' and 'the Faugh-a-Ballagh Boys' originated at the Battle of Barrosa. The 87th Regiment used this wild Irish battle-cry ('Clear the way') as they charged the enemy and so sealed the defeat of the French.

The Regiment has always marched to the stirring music of the Irish war pipes, which have the same chanter as the Scottish pipes, but only two drones.

THE CONNAUGHT RANGERS

PRECEDING TITLES

    1793   The 88th Regiment of Foot (Connaught Rangers)

    1881   The Connaught Rangers

TODAY

    The Regiment was disbanded in April 1922, when Ireland became a Republic.

NICKNAME

    The Devil's Own

REGIMENTAL MARCH

    (Not recorded)

THIS famous Regiment, the 88th Foot, was raised in Connaught on 25 September 1793 by Col the Hon. Thomas de Burgh (later the Earl of Clanrickard).

Its record of service can truthfully be said to be one of brilliant daring, high zeal, and an unselfish devotion to duty at all times. It earned its nickname by what seemed to be utter contempt for danger during the Peninsular War – it was Gen. Picton who first referred to the Regiment as 'the Devil's Own'. Wellington himself is reported as saying 'I don't know what effect [the 88th] will have upon the enemy, but, by God, they terrify me.' At Busaco the Regiment defeated a French force five times its own strength.

The 88th Regiment fought in Flanders under the Earl of Moira in 1794, and followed this by outstanding action in campaigns in the West Indies, India (1799), Egypt, and South America in 1806–8.

During World War I (1914–18) the Connaughts suffered

very heavy casualties on the Western Front and at Gallipoli. In 1920 the Regiment mutinied in India; it was
disbanded when the Irish Free State was founded in 1922.

The 89th Regiment of Foot

THE ROYAL IRISH FUSILIERS
(PRINCESS VICTORIA'S) – 2ND
BATTALION

PRECEDING TITLES
- 1793 The 89th Regiment of Foot
- 1866 The 89th (Princess Victoria's) Regiment of
  Foot
- 1881 2nd Battalion, Princess Victoria's (The Royal
  Irish Fusiliers)

TODAY
See The 87th Regiment of Foot.

NICKNAMES
Blarney's Blood-hounds
The Rollickers

REGIMENTAL MARCHES
'Garryowen'
'Barrosa'

THERE had been two Scottish regiments holding the
number '89', but both of these were disbanded in the
middle of the eighteenth century.

The Irish 89th Regiment was raised by Col William
Crosbie in the year 1793; Col Crosbie was later promoted
to Major-General.

After campaigning in Flanders, the Regiment served in

Ireland; it was there, during the 1798 Rebellion, that it gained the nickname 'Blarney's Blood-hounds', which refers to the tracking down of the Irish rebels. The historical reason for the name 'The Rollickers' is not recorded.

The Regiment next served at Malta (1801), and later gained the battle honour of the Sphinx superscribed 'Egypt' for its outstanding and distinguished service under Sir Ralph Abercromby at Alexandria.

The 89th served at Mauritius (1810), in Java (1811), and in Canada (1812–13); they also campaigned in India and Burma, and sailed for the Crimea from Cork in 1854.

In 1866 Her Majesty Queen Victoria presented a new stand of Colours to the Regiment. These replaced the Colours she had presented thirty three years previously when, as Princess Victoria, she was performing her first public ceremony.

The 90th Regiment of Foot

THE CAMERONIANS (SCOTTISH RIFLES) – 2ND BATTALION

PRECEDING TITLES

1794   The 90th, Perthshire Volunteers

1815   The 90th, Perthshire Light Infantry

1881   2nd Battalion, The Cameronians (Scottish Rifles)

TODAY

See the 26th Regiment of Foot

NICKNAME

The Perthshire Grey Breeks

'The Gathering of the Grahams'

THE 90th Foot, raised in 1794, had as its Colonel Thomas Graham, Laird of Balgowan: for his services at Barrosa in Spain during the Peninsular War (1811) Graham was made a peer and took the title Lord Lynedoch. At Barrosa Col Graham had found himself and the 90th Foot abandoned by the Spanish, but nevertheless he fought and defeated a vastly superior French force.

The Regiment's record of service includes the Egyptian campaign under Abercromby (1801). It also won battle honours marking distinguished service in the West Indies and the Crimea.

The 90th Foot became Light Infantry in 1815, and until 1881 remained the oldest surviving Light Infantry Regiment in the British Army.

Many of the original recruits of the 90th were among the toughest characters in Perthshire: some, in fact, were actually serving time in prison when they were recruited. The origin of their nickname may well be the fact that on enlistment many were still wearing their grey prison clothing.

The 26th, the 'Saintly' Cameronians, may have been a little taken aback on being given the 90th as their 2nd Battalion in 1881. But it is said that it was the men of the 90th Regiment who seemed the more upset: they continued to call themselves the 'Scottish Rifles'.

THE ARGYLL AND SUTHERLAND HIGHLANDERS (PRINCESS LOUISE'S)

PRECEDING TITLES

- 1794   The 98th (Argyllshire) Regiment of Foot
- 1798   The 91st (Argyllshire Highlanders) Regiment of Foot
- 1808   The 91st Regiment of Foot
- 1821   The 91st (Argyllshire) Highlanders
- 1872   The 91st (Princess Louise's) Argyllshire Highlanders
- 1881   Princess Louise's (Argyll and Sutherland) Highlanders
- 1921   The Argyll and Sutherland Highlanders (Princess Louise's)

TODAY

The Regiment is a component unit of the Scottish Division.

NICKNAME

The Rorys

REGIMENTAL MARCHES

'Bonnie Mary of Argyll'
'Highland Laddie'
'The Campbell March'

IN 1794 George III called for the raising of four regiments from the North. Among those chosen for this commission was the Duke of Argyll who, being in poor health, deputed Duncan Campbell of Lochnell to raise the Regiment, at first officially numbered the 98th. It was not until 1798 that it was promoted to being the 91st Foot.

The Argylls served in the Peninsular War with great

distinction, particularly at Corunna, and followed this by fighting at Waterloo. Later the Regiment did garrison duty at St Helena.

The Kaffir Wars were followed by service in Ireland (1851), and after ten years in India the Regiment went to South Africa again, this time to take part in the Zulu War (1879).

A draft of the 91st Regiment of Foot was part of the contingent which set such a heroic standard at the time of the wrecking of the *Birkenhead* (1852).

On a lighter note, the composer of the world-famous march 'Colonel Bogey' – Kenneth Alford – was once the Regimental Bandmaster of the Argyll and Sutherland Highlanders.

The 92nd Regiment of Foot

THE GORDON HIGHLANDERS – 2ND BATTALION

PRECEDING TITLES

1794   The 100th Regiment of Foot
1798   The 92nd Regiment of Foot
1861   The 92nd (Gordon Highlanders) Regiment
1881   The 2nd Battalion, The Gordon Highlanders

TODAY

See The 75th Regiment of Foot.

NICKNAME

The Gay Gordons

REGIMENTAL MARCH

'Cock of the North'

George, Marquis of Huntly and later fourth Duke of Gordon, raised a Highland Regiment in June 1794. This was numbered the 100th Regiment of Foot on embodiment, but although re-numbered the 92nd Regiment in 1798, was already known as the 'Gordon Highlanders'.

The first action was in Holland (1799), followed by service in Egypt under Sir Ralph Abercromby. Here the Regiment won the battle honour 'Mandora', as well as the Sphinx with the word 'Egypt' superscribed.

Next came the Peninsular War. The 92nd have a glorious record of activities in this campaign, gaining eight battle honours fighting under Sir John Moore and Sir Arthur Wellesley. They fought at Corunna where Sir John Moore was killed. In his memory the officers of the 92nd thereafter wore a black line in their lace, and it is said that the black buttons on their spats are also a tribute to his memory.

The 92nd Foot fought at Quatre Bras and at Waterloo. It was the 92nd who held on to the stirrups of the Royal Scots Greys in that famous charge at Waterloo.

The Crimea, the Indian Mutiny, the Afghan War – all saw the 92nd Regiment gaining more battle honours. The Regiment was linked with the 75th Regiment in 1881.

The 93rd Regiment of Foot

THE ARGYLL AND SUTHERLAND HIGHLANDERS (PRINCESS LOUISE'S) – 2ND BATTALION

PRECEDING TITLES

    1800   The 93rd Highlanders
    1861   The 93rd (Sutherland) Highlanders
    1881   2nd Battalion, Princess Louise's (Argyll and Sutherland) Highlanders

See The 91st Regiment of Foot.

The Thin Red Line

'The Thin Red Line'
'Highland Laddie'
'The Campbell March'

IN 1799 it was decided to raise a regular regiment of foot from Sutherland. The task was given to Maj.-Gen. William Wemyss of Wemyss, and the Regiment was embodied at Inverness in August 1800 and officially numbered '93'.

After service in the Channel Islands, Scotland, and Ireland, the Regiment was in action at the Cape of Good Hope, where it remained for eight years (1806–14). It served next in the West Indies and Canada; but it was in the Crimea (1854–6) that the 93rd earned its lasting title, 'The Thin Red Line'. After a distinguished performance at Alma, the 93rd was defending Balaclava against a large force of Russian cavalry. The Highlanders' line formation was two men deep, and held unbroken against repeated charges from the Russians – a thin red line tipped with steel.

The 93rd Foot was the only infantry regiment to bear the battle honour 'Balaclava' on its Colours.

The next important engagement was the Indian Mutiny (1858), where the 93rd fought with outstanding bravery at Lucknow. No less than seven Victoria Crosses were awarded to men of the 93rd for acts of heroism at this action.

THE CONNAUGHT RANGERS –
2ND BATTALION

PRECEDING TITLES
1823   The 94th Regiment of Foot
1881   2nd Battalion, The Connaught Rangers

TODAY
See The 88th Regiment of Foot.

NICKNAME
The Garvies

REGIMENTAL MARCH
(Not recorded)

IN all, four previous regiments had been allocated the number '94' as their designation. The Regiment later to become the 2nd Battalion, The Connaught Rangers, was raised in Glasgow in December 1823.

The 94th served in Gibraltar and Malta (1828–34), followed by fifteen years' continuous service in India; in fact a major portion of their operational career appears to be associated with that sub-continent.

The Regiment was back in England in 1854, but returned to Karachi in 1857 and served at Peshawar, on the North-West Frontier, and in central India until 1868.

In 1879 the Regiment was on active service against the Zulus; this was followed by the Boer War of 1880–1. As the 2nd Battalion the Connaught Rangers it was again posted to Malta (1889), Cyprus (1892), and Egypt (1895), serving with General Kitchener's Expeditionary Force (1896). This action was followed by a return to India in 1899.

THE SHERWOOD FORESTERS (NOTTINGHAM AND DERBYSHIRE) REGIMENT – 2ND BATTALION

PRECEDING TITLES

    1823   The 95th Regiment of Foot

    1825   The 95th, or Derbyshire Regiment of Foot

    1838   The 95th (Derbyshire) Regiment

    1881   2nd Battalion, The Sherwood Foresters (Derbyshire Regiment)

    1902   2nd Battalion, The Sherwood Foresters (Nottingham and Derbyshire) Regiment

TODAY

    See The 45th Regiment of Foot.

NICKNAMES

        The Nails

        The Sweeps

REGIMENTAL MARCHES

        'I'm Ninety-five'

        'The Derby Ram'

THE 95th Regiment of Foot was the sixth regiment to bear this number. It was raised at Winchester, and received its 'Derbyshire' title two years later.

In its first twenty years of service the Regiment saw action at Malta and in the Ionian Islands, Ceylon, and China.

The Crimean War saw the 95th in action in 1854. The Regiment fought with distinction at Alma, Inkerman, and at the siege of Sevastopol. These actions gave rise to comment from their Divisional Commander who said, 'There may be only a few of the 95th left, but those are as hard as nails!': this was said to be the origin of the nickname 'the Nails'.

When the Indian Mutiny broke out, the 95th Foot fought at Awah, Kotah, and other engagements. It was at Kotah that Pte McQuirt won the Regiment its first Victoria Cross.

It was also at Kotah that the 95th acquired a fighting ram as a mascot. The ram, known affectionately as 'Private Derby', marched nearly 3,000 miles with the Regiment through central India. After the Mutiny, Private Derby was awarded the India Medal – a replica of which his successors have continued to wear when appearing on parade.

It is appropriate to mention here that one of the previous 95th Regiments (removed from the Line in 1816) was titled the 95th Rifle Regiment, later to be called 'The Rifle Brigade'.

In this capacity, the Regiment is today a very active component unit of the 'large' regiment, The Royal Green Jackets of the Light Division.

The 96th Regiment of Foot

THE MANCHESTER REGIMENT – 2ND BATTALION

PRECEDING TITLES
    1824   The 96th Regiment of Foot
    1881   2nd Battalion, The Manchester Regiment

TODAY
    See The 63rd Regiment of Foot.

    The Bendovers

    'The Manchester'

ALTHOUGH the Preceding Titles list above covers only the Regiment permanently established as the 96th Regiment of Foot in 1824, it is worth recording that there had been four previous regiments numbered '96', all having some connection with the Eighth, or King's Regiment. Their titles are recorded as follows:

1761   96th Regiment of Foot, disbanded 1763.

1779   96th Foot (The British Musqueteers), disbanded 1783.

1793   Re-formed as above, and disbanded in 1796.

1798   The Minorca Regiment, renumbered The 97th Foot (The Queen's German Regiment).

1812   Retitled The Queen's Own (Royal) Regiment.

1816   Re-numbered The 96th Foot. Disbanded 1818.

It is interesting to note that two of the battle honours held by the present 96th Foot were inherited from the last of the temporary Regiments of that title.

The present Regiment was raised at Manchester in 1824 as the 96th Regiment of Foot; and it retained its connection with that city. It was in fact this connection which resulted in the name 'The Manchester Regiment' when the 96th was linked with the 63rd Regiment of Foot in 1881.

The 96th served in North America (1825–35), and followed this by garrison duty in New South Wales(1840); it was from there that it went on to play a prominent part in the Maori War of 1846–7. Then followed several years of service in India, broken by two short periods of duty at the Cape (1855) and at Gibraltar (1857).

136

THE QUEEN'S OWN (ROYAL WEST KENT) REGIMENT – 2ND BATTALION

PRECEDING TITLES
- 1825 The 97th Regiment of Foot
- 1826 The 97th, or Earl of Ulster's Regiment
- 1881 The 2nd Battalion, The Queen's Own (Royal West Kent) Regiment

TODAY
See The 50th Regiment of Foot.

NICKNAME
The Celestials

REGIMENTAL MARCH
'Men of Kent'

THE 97th Regiment of Foot was raised at Winchester in 1825 by Maj.-Gen. Sir James Lyon; the following year it was granted the subsidiary title 'The Earl of Ulster's Regiment'.

The Regiment served in Ceylon, the Mediterranean, Canada, and Greece, following this by fighting in the Crimea in 1854. It endured the terrible winter Siege of Sevastopol – for acts of valour two members of the Regiment were awarded the V.C. The 97th led the assault on the Redan, and of the 360 officers and men at that action, 212 became casualties.

The Regiment went to India in 1857, and in the following year played a major part in the bitter fighting at Lucknow.

The nickname of the Regiment is of considerable interest:

137

the uniform had facings of a 'heavenly blue', and so it was known as 'the Celestials'. In fact, the facings were the blue of the ribbon of the Order of Saint Patrick, an Order worn by the first Colonel, the Earl of Ulster.

The 98th Regiment of Foot

THE NORTH STAFFORDSHIRE REGIMENT (THE PRINCE OF WALES'S) – 2ND BATTALION

PRECEDING TITLES
 1824 The 98th Regiment of Foot
 1876 The 98th (The Prince of Wales's) Regiment
 1881 The 2nd Battalion, The North Staffordshire Regiment (The Prince of Wales's)

TODAY
 See The 64th Regiment of Foot.

NICKNAME
 The Powos

REGIMENTAL MARCH
 'God Bless the Prince of Wales'

THERE were five previous 98th Regiments of Foot. The one under discussion was raised at Chichester in 1824 with Maj.-Gen. Henry Conran as Colonel and Col Mildmay-Fane as Lieutenant-Colonel and Commanding Officer.

In 1825 the Regiment was sent to South Africa and remained there for some twelve years, its main duty being the guarding of the white settlers. The Commanding Officer at that time was Lt-Col Colin Campbell.

Police duties in England and Ireland were the next phase of the Regiment's service.

In 1842 the 98th Foot were serving in China and had the misfortune to suffer the loss of some sixty per cent of their strength, mostly by death from heat-stroke and disease.

The Regiment was in India at the time of the Mutiny (1858) but most of the time was spent on guard duty on the North-West Frontier.

The 99th Regiment of Foot

THE WILTSHIRE REGIMENT (DUKE OF EDINBURGH'S) – 2ND BATTALION

PRECEDING TITLES

    1824   The 99th Regiment of Foot
    1832   The 99th (Lanarkshire) Regiment of Foot
    1874   The 99th, or Duke of Edinburgh's Regiment
    1881   2nd Battalion, The Wiltshire Regiment (Duke of Edinburgh's)

TODAY

    See The 62nd Regiment of Foot.

NICKNAME

        The Queen's Pets

REGIMENTAL MARCHES

        'Blue Bonnets over the Border'
        'Point of War'
        'Auld Robin Grey' (slow)

THE 99th Regiment of Foot was originally raised in Glasgow by Maj.-Gen. Gage John Hall in 1824.

It was during its service in South Africa (1868) that H.R.H. Prince Alfred, Duke of Edinburgh (second son of Queen Victoria) became associated with the Regiment. In 1874 it was given the Duke's title, and incorporated his cypher and coronet on the Colours.

Right up to 1881 the Regiment maintained its association with its Scottish Lowland origin, wearing a diced border on the shako and forage cap.

The 99th Foot was renowned for its smartness of appearance and drill; in 1858, while stationed at Aldershot, it was always chosen to guard the Royal Pavilion – hence the nickname 'the Queen's Pets'.

Another interesting story arises from the Regiment's smartness of dress: other regiments at Aldershot were always trying to achieve the same level of appearance as the 99th, which endeavours are said to have given rise to the expression 'dressed up to the nines'.

The 100th Regiment of Foot

THE PRINCE OF WALES'S LEINSTER REGIMENT (ROYAL CANADIANS)

PRECEDING TITLES

1858 The 100th (Prince of Wales's Royal Canadian) Regiment

1881 The Prince of Wales's Leinster Regiment (Royal Canadians)

TODAY

The Regiment was disbanded in April 1922, when Ireland became a Republic.

The Beavers   The Maple Leaves

The Colonials   The Old Hundred

The Centipedes

REGIMENTAL MARCHES

'The Royal Canadians'

'God Bless the Prince of Wales'

FIVE previous regiments, all since disbanded, held the number '100', including a Scottish regiment raised by Major Colin Campbell at Stirling in 1761.

The present 100th Regiment owes its existence to the surge of loyalty which swept Canada, then a colony, at the time of the Indian Mutiny. However, by the time the Regiment was ready for embarkation, the mutiny had been subdued: instead, the Royal Canadians went to Gibraltar in 1858, and to Malta in 1869. They then went to India and remained there on normal garrison duty until 1095.

It is interesting to note that the 100th Regiment was the last British regiment to serve in Canada, as well as being the only British regiment to carry a colonial title.

The 101st Regiment of Foot

THE ROYAL MUNSTER FUSILIERS

PRECEDING TITLES

1756 The Bengal European Regiment (Honourable East India Company)

1840 The 1st Bengal (European) Regiment

1841 The 1st Bengal (European) Light Infantry

1846 The 1st Bengal (European) Fusiliers

1858 The 1st Bengal Fusiliers

1861 The 101st, Royal Bengal Fusiliers

1881 The Royal Munster Fusiliers

The Regiment was disbanded in 1922, on the foundation of the Irish Free State.

The Dirty Shirts

'The Boys of Wexford'

THIS famous Regiment was able to trace its origin back to 1756, when it was raised and served under the direction of The Honourable East India Company. Four other regiments, all since disbanded, carried the number '101', including a Scottish regiment named Johnston's Highlanders (1760–3).

The Regiment served with Abercromby against the Rohillas (an Afghan tribe), and then took part in the campaigns of Lord Lake in the Mahratta War (1803–5). It was at the occupation of Macao in 1809, and served with great distinction in the first Sikh War (1846), and the Burma War of 1851–3.

During the Indian Mutiny the 101st Regiment fought in their shirt sleeves at the Siege of Delhi – this, it is said, was the origin of the nickname 'Dirty Shirts'.

While they were stationed at Rawalpindi the Regiment took part in the Ambela campaign of 1863, returning to England in 1868.

The 102nd Regiment of Foot

THE ROYAL DUBLIN FUSILIERS

PRECEDING TITLES

1648   The Madras European Regiment

1702   The Honourable East India Company's European Regiment

1830   The Honourable East India Company's Madras (European) Regiment

1843   The 1st Madras (European) Fusiliers

1858   The 1st Madras Fusiliers

1862   The 102nd, Royal Madras Fusiliers

1881   The Royal Dublin Fusiliers

TODAY

The Regiment was disbanded in 1922, on the foundation of the Irish Free State.

NICKNAMES

The Blue-caps

The Lambs

REGIMENTAL MARCH

'St Patrick's Day'

THIS famous Regiment could trace its history back to 1648, when a small company of fifty men was recruited to man the wall surrounding a brick factory, which was later to become Fort St George, the foundation of the city of Madras.

In 1664 the garrison was increased, and in 1683 an experienced Ensign was sent from Madras, with thirty soldiers, to Hoogly in Bengal – later to become the city of Calcutta. In 1703 the enlistment of a woman is recorded.

Robert Clive, described as a clerk, aged 19, arrived at Fort St George in 1744; he was later to become C.O. of the Madras Regiment, and defeat the French supporting Chanda Sahib at Arcot, a name which became the first battle honour inscribed on the Regimental Colour.

In April 1756 came the news of the 'Black Hole of Calcutta'. Clive's avenging army included drafts of the Madras European Regiment; defeating the French and the Nawab's armies at Plassey, it secured Bengal for the British Empire.

The Madras Regiment fought at Pondicherry, and secured more battle honours at Nundygroog and Bangalore in 1791. Then came service in the Mahratta and Burmese Wars (1851), and the Sikh Wars of 1846–8.

The Regiment became fusiliers in 1843; it was given a 'Royal' title in 1862. It won four V.C.s during the Indian Mutiny. The nickname 'Blue-caps' came from the regimental head-gear, which became as well known to the enemy as did the 'Red Berets' of World War II, and for very similar reasons.

The 103rd Regiment of Foot

THE ROYAL DUBLIN FUSILIERS – 2ND BATTALION

PRECEDING TITLES

- 1661 The Bombay Regiment
- 1668 The Honourable East India Company's Bombay (European) Regiment
- 1844 The 1st Bombay (European) Fusiliers
- 1859 The 1st Bombay Fusiliers
- 1862 The 103rd, Royal Bombay Fusiliers
- 1881 2nd Battalion, The Royal Dublin Fusiliers

See The 102nd Regiment of Foot.

The Old Toughs

'Let Erin Remember'

IN 1661 was recruited the Bombay Regiment, which became the ancestor of the 2nd Battalion, The Royal Dublin Fusiliers.

England acquired the port and island of Bombay when Charles II married the Infanta Catherine of Braganza; in 1668 the King transferred the island of Bombay to The Honourable East India Company.

The Bombay Regiment fought at Trichinopoly and with Clive at Plassey, so helping in the overthrow of French power in India.

In the Bednore campaign (1783) against Tippoo Sahib, the Bombay European Regiment suffered the severe loss of eleven officers and 300 men: later, however, it again fought against Tippoo under Sir Arthur Wellesley, and defeated him at Seringapatam (1799).

In 1821 the Bombay Europeans campaigned in Arabia, capturing Aden in 1839; as fusiliers they fought in the Sikh Wars and in the Indian Mutiny.

The Regiment became the 103rd Regiment of the Line in 1862, the same year that the Madras Fusiliers became the 102nd. In 1873 the two Regiments were linked together by a joint Brigade Depot at Naas in County Kildare, Ireland. Finally, in 1881, the old Bombay Fusiliers were linked with the old 1st Madras Fusiliers to form the Royal Dublin Fusiliers.

The nickname 'Old Toughs' is said to have originated as a tribute to the Regiment's span of over two hundred years of service in India.

THE ROYAL MUNSTER FUSILIERS – 2ND BATTALION

PRECEDING TITLES
- 1839   The 2nd Bengal (European) Regiment, The Honourable East India Company
- 1850   The 2nd (Bengal European) Fusiliers
- 1858   The 2nd Bengal Fusiliers
- 1861   The 104th, Bengal Fusiliers
- 1881   2nd Battalion, The Royal Munster Fusiliers

TODAY

See The 101st Regiment of Foot.

NICKNAME

The Lambs

REGIMENTAL MARCH

'The Boys of Wexford'

THE 104th Regiment of Foot was originally raised in 1839 by The Honourable East India Company as the 2nd Bengal (European) Regiment. It acted in a major role as part of Gen. Gilbert's Division in the second Sikh War (1849), and, as the 2nd (Bengal European) Fusiliers, embarked for Burma and fought with great distinction in the second Burma War (1852).

The Regiment fought in the Indian Mutiny, and, together with the 101st Foot, to which it was later linked, played a major part in the Siege of Delhi.

It came home to England in 1871, and after linking with the 101st Regiment by becoming the 2nd Battalion, The Royal Munster Fusiliers, served for a time in Malta (1882), following this by a return to Madras.

THE KING'S OWN YORKSHIRE LIGHT INFANTRY – 2ND BATTALION

PRECEDING TITLES

- 1839   The 2nd Madras (European Light Infantry) Regiment
- 1858   The 2nd Madras (Light Infantry) Regiment
- 1861   The 105th Regiment of Foot (Madras Light Infantry)
- 1881   2nd Battalion, The King's Own Light Infantry (South Yorkshire Regiment)
- 1887   2nd Battalion, The King's Own (Yorkshire Light Infantry)

TODAY

See The 51st Regiment of Foot.

NICKNAME

The Koylis

REGIMENTAL MARCH

'The Jockey of York'

THREE previous regiments, all since disbanded, carried the number '105'. One was a Scottish regiment raised by Col David Graeme at Perth in 1762.

The present Regiment was raised by The Honourable East India Company in July 1839. The first Colonel was Archibald Brown-Dyce, and the first headquarters was at Arnee.

After a brief period of service in Burma (1856), the Regiment fought in the Indian Mutiny. This was followed by the general transference of the East India Company's regiments to the British Army. The 2nd Madras Regiment became the 105th Foot (1861).

Following a spell of active service in Aden (1872), the

Regiment came to England for its first home service tour of duty.

After linking with the 51st Foot (1881) the 105th saw service at Malta, Quetta, and Baluchistan, as well as outstanding action on the North-West Frontier against Afridi tribesmen.

The 106th Regiment of Foot

THE DURHAM LIGHT INFANTRY – 2ND BATTALION

PRECEDING TITLES

<blockquote>

1839   The Honourable East India Company's 2nd Bombay European Infantry Regiment

1858   The 2nd Bombay European Light Infantry

1862   The 106th Bombay Light Infantry

1881   2nd Battalion, The Durham Light Infantry

</blockquote>

TODAY

See The 68th Regiment of Foot.

NICKNAME

(None recorded)

REGIMENTAL MARCH

'The Keel Row'

THE Honourable East India Company had a number of regiments serving in India which, after the Company was abolished in 1858, were taken over by the British Army.

The 106th Foot, raised in 1839 as the 2nd Bombay European Infantry, later became a Light Infantry regiment and served in the Persian War of 1856–7.

The Regiment came under the control of the British Army in 1862, after the Indian Mutiny, and as the 106th

148

Bombay Light Infantry continued to serve in India for the next ten years.

It was not until 1873 that the Regiment came to England and raised recruits alongside the 68th Foot, which in 1881 became its senior regiment. The battle honours of the 106th were then added to those of the 68th, the uniform was modified, and the two Battalions shared a common depot at Sunderland.

The 107th Regiment of Foot

THE ROYAL SUSSEX REGIMENT – 2ND BATTALION

PRECEDING TITLES

1854   The 2nd Bengal (European) Light Infantry (Honourable East India Company)
1858   The 2nd Bengal Light Infantry
1862   The 107th, Bengal Infantry
1881   2nd Battalion, The Royal Sussex Regiment

TODAY

See the 35th Regiment of Foot.

NICKNAME

(None recorded)

REGIMENTAL MARCHES

'The Lass of Richmond Hill'
'Sussex by the Sea'

THE original 2nd Battalion of the Royal Sussex Regiment was raised in 1799, and after service in Holland, distinguished itself at the capture of Malta. It is said that the Maltese Cross in the regimental badge is a reminder of the part played by the 2nd Battalion in this particular engagement.

After Waterloo and the subsequent victory parade the 2nd Battalion was disbanded.

It was not until after the Indian Mutiny that the Royal Sussex Regiment acquired as a 2nd Battalion the 107th Bengal Infantry. This unit, which had already given outstanding service in the Mutiny, had originally been raised by The Honourable East India Company as the 2nd Bengal (European) Light Infantry in 1854. This 2nd Battalion served in India for many years after the Mutiny, mostly on the North-West Frontier.

The 108th Regiment of Foot

THE ROYAL INNISKILLING FUSILIERS – 2ND BATTALION

PRECEDING TITLES

    1854   The 3rd Madras European Regiment (The Honourable East India Company)

    1862   The 108th (Madras Infantry) Regiment

    1881   2nd Battalion, The Royal Inniskilling Fusiliers

TODAY

    See The 27th Regiment of Foot.

NICKNAME

       The Lumps

REGIMENTAL MARCHES

       'The British Grenadiers'

       'Sprig of Shillelagh'

THIS Regiment was raised in India by the Honourable East India Company in 1854 and for several years served in central India on Company duty, eventually becoming the Company's 108th (Madras Infantry) Regiment in 1862. It fought with great distinction in the Indian Mutiny.

In 1881 the Regiment linked with the 27th Regiment, The Royal Inniskilling Fusiliers. At the same time the Inniskillings also absorbed the Fermanagh, Royal Tyrone, Londonderry, and Donegal Militias.

As the 2nd Battalion, The Royal Inniskilling Fusiliers, the unit was stationed in Malta in the early part of 1886; in 1888 it went to India, and served with some distinction as part of the Peshawar Column under Gen. Sir William Lockard (1897–8).

The 109th Regiment of Foot

THE PRINCE OF WALES'S LEINSTER REGIMENT (ROYAL CANADIANS) – 2ND BATTALION

PRECEDING TITLES
- 1854   The 3rd Bombay European Regiment (Honourable East India Company)
- 1858   The 3rd (Bombay) Regiment
- 1861   The 109th (Bombay Infantry) Regiment
- 1881   2nd Battalion, The Prince of Wales's Leinster Regiment (Royal Canadians)

TODAY

See the 100th Regiment of Foot

NICKNAMES

The Poona Pets	The Wild Indians
The Brass Heads	The German Mob
The Crusaders	

'The Royal Canadians'
'Come back to Erin'

THIS Regiment was raised in 1854 by The Honourable East India Company; it was recruited mainly from volunteers from the 1st Bombay Fusiliers, the 2nd Bombay Light Infantry, and men drafted from The Honourable East India Company's depot at Worley, Essex.

The Regiment served as the Central India Field Force in 1857, and it was during this period that the nickname 'The Brass Heads' was earned: so good was the physique of the men in the Regiment that they seemed to be completely indifferent to the blazing sun and the heat of central India.

The Regiment took part in the Baroda engagements and fought at the Relief of Sanger; it was here that Pte Whirlpool won the Victoria Cross at Muddenpore Pass.

While based at Aden (1865-6) the Regiment took part in two expeditions into Arabia against the Sultan Abdallah, and gave very distinguished service at Bir Said. It returned to India in 1877, and was finally linked with the 100th Foot in 1881.

What became of the regiments of foot

A table showing the various amalgamations, from the numbered regiments to the present divisions

'Large' and unchanged regiments are printed in bold type; disbanded regiments are printed in italics.

The King's Division

Regiments of Foot

No.	Regiment		Amalgamated
4	The King's Own Royal Regiment (Lancaster)	}	**The King's Own Royal Border Regiment**
34, 55	The Border Regiment		
8	The King's Regiment (Liverpool)	}	**The King's Regiment (Manchester and Liverpool)**
63, 96	The Manchester Regiment		
30, 59	The East Lancashire Regiment / The Lancashire Regiment (Prince of Wales's Volunteers)	}	**The Queen's Lancashire Regiment (Loyals and Lancashire)**
40, 82	The South Lancashire Regiment (Prince of Wales's Volunteers)		
47, 81	The Loyal Regiment (North Lancashire)		
14	The West Yorkshire Regiment (The Prince of Wales's Own)	}	**The Prince of Wales's Own Regiment of Yorkshire**
15	The East Yorkshire Regiment (The Duke of York's Own)		
19	**The Green Howards (Alexandra, Princess of Wales's Own Yorkshire Regiment)**		
33, 76	**The Duke of Wellington's Regiment (West Riding)**		
65, 84	*The York and Lancaster Regiment*		
27, 108	The Royal Inniskilling Fusiliers	}	**The Royal Irish Rangers**
83, 86	The Royal Ulster Rifles		
87, 89	The Royal Irish Fusiliers (Princess Victoria's)		

Regiments of Foot			
2	The Queen's Royal Regiment (West Surrey)	} The Queen's Royal Surrey Regiment	
31	The East Surrey Regiment		
70			
3	The Buffs (Royal East Kent Regiment)	}	**The Queen's Regiment**
50	The Queen's Own Royal West Kent Regiment	}	
97			
35	The Royal Sussex Regiment		
107			
57	The Middlesex Regiment (Duke of Cambridge's Own)	}	
77			
5	The Royal Northumberland Fusiliers		**The Royal Regiment of Fusiliers**
6	The Royal Warwickshire Regiment		
7	The Royal Fusiliers (City of London Regiment)		
20	*The Lancashire Fusiliers*		
9	The Royal Norfolk Regiment	} The First East Anglian Regiment (Royal Norfolk and Suffolk)	
12	The Suffolk Regiment		
10	The Royal Lincolnshire Regiment	} The Second East Anglian Regiment (Duchess of Gloucester's Own Royal Lincolnshire and Northamptonshire)	**The Royal Anglian Regiment**
48	The Northamptonshire Regiment		
58			
16	The Bedfordshire and Hertfordshire Regiment	} The Third East Anglian Regiment	
44	The Essex Regiment		
56			
17	*The Royal Leicestershire Regiment*		

MRF

The Prince of Wales's Division

Regiments of Foot		First merger	Final regiment
11		The Devonshire Regiment	The Devonshire and Dorset Regiment
39 54		The Dorset Regiment	
28 61			The Gloucestershire Regiment
37 67			The Royal Hampshire Regiment
49 66		The Royal Berkshire Regiment (Princess Charlotte of Wales's)	The Duke of Edinburgh's Royal Regiment (Berkshire and Wiltshire)
62 99		The Wiltshire Regiment (The Duke of Edinburgh's)	
38 80		The South Staffordshire Regiment	The Staffordshire Regiment (The Prince of Wales's)
64 98		The North Staffordshire Regiment (The Prince of Wales's)	
22			The Cheshire Regiment
29 36		The Worcestershire Regiment	The Worcestershire and Sherwood Foresters Regiment
45 95		The Sherwood Foresters (Nottingham and Derbyshire Regiment)	
24		The South Wales Borderers	The Royal Regiment of Wales
41 69		The Welch Regiment	
23			The Royal Welch Fusiliers

The Scottish Division

The Light Division

The Light Division

Regiments of Foot			
13	The Somerset Light Infantry (Prince Albert's) } The Somerset and Cornwall Light Infantry		
32, 46	The Duke of Cornwall's Light Infantry }		
51, 105	The King's Own Yorkshire Light Infantry	The Light Infantry	
68, 106	The Durham Light Infantry		
53, 85	The King's Shropshire Light Infantry }		
43, 52	The Oxfordshire and Buckinghamshire Light Infantry } The Royal Green Jackets		
60	The King's Royal Rifle Corps }		
—	The Rifle Brigade		

Irish Regiments

disbanded on the foundation of the Irish Free State in 1922

Regiments
of Foot

18 The Royal Irish Regiment

88 ⎫
94 ⎭ The Connaught Rangers

100 ⎫
109 ⎭ The Prince of Wales's Leinster Regiment (Royal Canadians)

101 ⎫
104 ⎭ The Royal Munster Fusiliers

102 ⎫
103 ⎭ The Royal Dublin Fusiliers

INDEX

Note. To index fully the detail contained in this book would require double the space available. This index is therefore necessarily a *selective* one; it contains entries to the names of the regiments of foot (with cross-references where appropriate), officers and men mentioned in the text, battles and campaigns fought and places where the regiments have served. Regrettably it has not been possible to include nicknames, regimental marches, colours, battle honours, badges, mascots, preceding titles or places where the regiments were raised; this information will be found in the text under each regiment individually. Furthermore, no entries appear in the index concerning the composition of present divisions; these are listed in the tables following page 152.

Augusta, Princess, 45
Austrian Succession, War of the, 49, 65, 71
Awah, 135

Badajos, 46, 59, 119, 121
Baird, Sir David, 87
Balaclava, vi, 132
Baluchistan, 148
Bangalore, 107, 144
Barcelona, 53
Baroda, 152
Barrington, Col the Hon. John, 94
Barrosa, 124, 128
Bastia, 46
Bath, Earl of (John Grenville), 16
Bayonne, 110
Bedfordshire and Hertfordshire Regiment, 25–6, 65
Bednore, 145
Bengal, 143, 144
Berkshire and Wiltshire, see Duke of Edinburgh's Royal Regiment
Bertie, Col Albermarle (6th Earl of Lindsay), 116
Bidassoa, 110
Bir Said, 152
Birkenhead (troop-ship), 11, 20, 64, 106, 107, 130
Black Watch (Royal Highland Regiment), 62–3
2nd Battalion, 105–6
Blenheim, 14, 16, 24, 26, 33, 36, 37, 40
Bloody Assizes, 7
Boer War, 1st, 86, 133
Border Regiment, 6, 51–2
2nd Battalion, 81–2
Bombay, 119, 145
Boscawen, Admiral Edward, 45
Boston Massacre, 45
Bouchain, 33
Bourbon, 123
Boyne, the, 10, 15, 35, 36
Bragg, Col Philip, 43
Brandywine, 36, 69, 73, 92

Brest, 4
Bristol, 18
Brooklyn, 92
Brown-Dyce, Col Archibald, 147
Brussels, 113
Buckingham, 1st Marquis of, 121
'Buff Howards', 6
Buffs, The, 4–6, 30, 74, 89
Bunker's Hill, 36, 64, 87, 92, 95
Burgos, 86
Burma, 21, 35, 82, 127, 146, 147
Burmese Wars, 14, 29, 67, 115, 142, 144, 146
Busaco, 67, 119, 125
Byng, Admiral John, 12
Byrne, Pte John, 99

Cadiz, 49, 54
Calcutta, 143, 144
Calvert, Sir Harry, 26
Calvi, 76
Cameron, Richard, 40
Cameron of Erracht, Major (later Lt-Gen. Sir) Alan, 113
Cameronian Sect, 40
Cameronians (Scottish Rifles), 39–40
2nd Battalion, 127–8
Campbell, Lt-Col Colin, 138
Campbell, Major Colin, 141
Campbell, Col John (5th Duke of Argyll), 80, 129
Campbell of Inverniel, Sir Archibald, 107
Campbell of Lochnell, Duncan, 129
Canada, 26, 35, 39, 43, 49, 63, 65, 67, 69, 70, 82, 88, 91, 98, 105, 111, 116, 118, 120, 127, 132, 137, 141
Canton, 87
Cape of Good Hope, 87, 112, 116, 122, 132, 136
Captain, H.M.S., 100
Cardwell, Viscount, vi
Cardwell Reforms, vi, 62, 72, 106, 114

169